C000235761

Andrew D. Mayes is Spirituality Advi:
where he served as Director of Cont
He has an international teaching .
Yale Divinity School and Virginia Theological Seminary. He teaches
regularly at St George's College Jerusalem, where he has been
Course Director. This is his fifth book with SPCK, complement-
ing *Holy Land?* (2011) and *Beyond the Edge* (2013). It is a sequel to
Spirituality in Ministerial Formation (University of Wales Press, 2009).

ANOTHER CHRIST

Re-envisioning ministry

Andrew D. Mayes

First published in Great Britain in 2014

Society for Promoting Christian Knowledge
36 Causton Street
London SW1P 4ST
www.spckpublishing.co.uk

Copyright © Andrew D. Mayes 2014

All rights reserved. No part of this book may be reproduced or transmitted in any form or by any
means, electronic or mechanical, including photocopying, recording, or by any information
storage and retrieval system, without permission in writing from the publisher.

SPCK does not necessarily endorse the individual views contained in its publications.

The author and publisher have made every effort to ensure that the external website and email
addresses included in this book are correct and up to date at the time of going to press. The author
and publisher are not responsible for the content, quality or continuing accessibility of the sites.

Unless otherwise noted, Scripture quotations are taken from the New Revised Standard Version of
the Bible, Anglicized Edition, copyright © 1989, 1995 by the Division of Christian Education of the
National Council of the Churches of Christ in the USA. Used by permission. All rights reserved.
Quotations marked RSV are from the Revised Standard Version of the Bible, copyright © 1946,
1952 and 1971 by the Division of Christian Education of the National Council of the
Churches of Christ in the USA. Used by permission. All rights reserved.
Quotations marked ESV are from The Holy Bible, English Standard Version, copyright © 2001
by Crossway Bibles, a division of Good News Publishers. Used by permission. All rights reserved.
Quotations marked NIV are taken from the Holy Bible, New International Version (Anglicized
edition). Copyright © 1979, 1984, 2011 by Biblica (formerly International Bible Society). Used by
permission of Hodder & Stoughton Publishers, an Hachette UK company. All rights reserved.
'NIV' is a registered trademark of Biblica (formerly International Bible Society).
UK trademark number 1448790.

The publisher and author acknowledge with thanks permission to reproduce extracts
from the following:
Extracts from *Common Worship* are copyright © The Archbishops' Council, 2000,
and are reproduced by permission. <copyright@churchofengland.org>
Common Worship: Ordination Services is copyright © The Archbishops' Council, 2006,
and extracts are reproduced by permission. <copyright@churchofengland.org>
'Spirit of the Living God' by Daniel Iverson is copyright © 1935, renewed 1963 Birdwing
Music (Adm. CapitolCMGPublishing.com/Small Stone Media BV/Song Solutions.
<www.songsolutions.org>). All rights reserved. Used by permission.
Every effort has been made to seek permission to use copyright material reproduced in this
book. The publisher apologizes for those cases where permission might not have been
sought and, if notified, will formally seek permission at the earliest opportunity.

British Library Cataloguing-in-Publication Data
A catalogue record for this book is available from the British Library

ISBN 978–0–281–07246–0
eBook ISBN 978–0–281–07247–7

Typeset by Graphicraft Limited, Hong Kong
First printed in Great Britain by Ashford Colour Press
Subsequently digitally printed in Great Britain

eBook by Graphicraft Limited, Hong Kong

Produced on paper from sustainable forests

Contents

———◆•◆•◆———

Introduction

————•◆•————

Spiritual formation for leaders: formed into his likeness?

In all traditions of ministry and priesthood, the call is to become more like Jesus Christ. Some traditions envision the priest as an *alter Christus*, another Christ. They talk of the priest acting *in persona Christi*. Others are inspired by the *Imitatio Christi*, the imitation of Christ. Priestly formation or ministerial growth is thought of in terms of an increase in Christlikeness. A classic manual in one tradition was called *Christ: The Ideal of the Priest*.[1]

The Pauline writings employ the language of continuous transformation into Christ: 'Do not be conformed to this world, but be *transformed* by the renewing of your minds' (Rom. 12.2). Paul teaches that Christians' calling and vocation, indeed destiny, is 'to be *conformed* to the image of his Son' (Rom. 8.29). As John Ziesler puts it: 'Bearing his image is being like him, and representing him.'[2] The Greek idea *summorphosis* means 'to be formed or fashioned like, to be shaped like'. Inner lives are to be reshaped according to the pattern of Christ; personal resources and aptitudes to be realigned to the template of Christ.

If this growth in Christlikeness is a goal for all Christians, it is especially so for those in ministry or leadership. Paul puts it: 'My little children, for whom I am again in the pain of childbirth until Christ be formed [*morphothe*] in you' (Gal. 4.19). John develops this in terms of *homoiosis* or assimilation to God (1 John 3.2). The Catholic tradition speaks of the need for the priest's total identification with Christ, a reconfiguration of the person in accordance with Christ.[3]

A crucial question

'Form us into the likeness of Christ', we pray.[4] But what image of Christ is in view? What image of Christ are Christian leaders, deacons and priests invited to reproduce in their ministry? The Anglican Ordinal offers only two models of Christ to inspire a lifetime of ministry. For priests it invites a reshaping of candidates' lives on the model of Christ the Good Shepherd: 'They are to set the example of the Good Shepherd always before them as the pattern of their calling.'[5] For deacons Christ the servant is the recommended model: 'In the name of our Lord, we bid you remember the greatness of the trust in which you are now to share: the ministry of Christ himself, who for our sake took the form of a servant' (Declarations). The example of Christ's footwashing of the disciples is mentioned three times in the service of ordination of deacons: 'as he washed the feet of his disciples, so they must wash the feet of others'. No other picture of ministry is offered. This is as good as it gets! Books on servant leadership abound.[6]

But these images of Christ to which we are invited to be conformed have become safe and traditional and predictable. They have become institutional norms: clergy are summoned to be increasingly like Christ servant and shepherd, and maintain the existing Church more or less successfully. They refer to a model of faithful pastoral ministry that seems to allow no scope for innovation or eccentricity. The ordination gives only this vision of ministry: 'Priests are called to be servants and shepherds among the people to whom they are sent.'

But what if clergy were to look for inspiration in their leadership to recent rediscoveries of the person of Christ? William Willimon identifies courage as a key quality to be developed in today's Christian leadership and clergy. In *Calling and Character: Virtues of the Ordained Life* he is critical of how clergy have become a respectable profession accommodated to the spirit of the age: 'We seem to have a high proportion of those who wish to keep house, to conform, and too few who like to play, confront, disrupt, revise, and foolishly envision.'[7] He calls on theological educators to seek to form clergy who can dare to be subversive, unsettling in their prophetic and countercultural witness. He is one rare voice, among others, who suggests that we might be inspired by another Christ. It might turn out to make a difference!

Origins of this book

This book originates from two milieux. One is 30 years of parish ministry, during which I have served as priest in a diversity of settings, for eight years responsible for clergy training and ongoing formation in a large diocese. In the midst of this I could see the need both for models of ministry that inspire and hearten and for a spirituality that energizes, sustains and sometimes upsets and disturbs ministry.

The other setting of this book was working for some time as Course Director at St George's College Jerusalem, to which I am connected as an associate professor. I led groups around the Holy Land, going in search of the historical Jesus and his first-century setting. I encountered both the latest scholarship on the historical person of Jesus and the physical setting of his ministry: the towns, valleys, mountains and terrain, which I have explored in two other books.[8] I was struck by surprising images of Jesus – that were not part of the traditional teaching on Christology. We had studied Jesus as Son of God, Son of Man, Messiah, Saviour, Judge, King. But now I was discovering startling and refreshing images of Jesus that I had not met before. New researches into the social and cultural background of the first century, anthropological and sociological, have brought significant new insights to the question of the identity and work of Jesus of Nazareth. I was realizing that these academic investigations had extraordinary implications for the practice of ministry. As Hugh Anderson puts it:

> it is incumbent on us in our secular age to try to show Christian believers and unbelievers alike that the Christology question is not simply a matter of esoteric debate . . . within the academy, but relates directly to the practical experience of men and women in their lived world . . . the experiential or existential dimension in New Testament Christology or, if you like, its relationship to and implications for the human situation, is congenial to . . . the necessity of wedding theory and praxis (action).[9]

Moreover, there was something paradoxically earthy and transcendent about these new – or ancient and forgotten – images of Jesus. They were intensely human but shot through with divinity. They are the basis of this new book. Jesus emerges as one who is gutsy, provocative, feisty – not 'gentle Jesus meek and mild' but one who is forever breaking out of boxes and titles. C. S. Lewis puts it: 'He's wild, you know. Not like a tame lion.'[10]

This book is a third part of a trilogy and also a sequel – but stands on its own. In *Holy Land? Challenging Questions from the Biblical Landscape* (London: SPCK, 2011) I sought to help the reader grapple with tough questions arising from the terrain of the Holy Land, and in *Beyond the Edge: Spiritual Transitions for Adventurous Souls* (London: SPCK, 2013) I explored how Jesus' call, 'Follow me', leads us into liminal spaces where we are likely to be undone before we are remade and reshaped by Christ. In this third book we see how the first-century setting of Jesus, and his identities within them, suggest a fresh look at ministry today. As a sequel to *Spirituality in Ministerial Formation: The Dynamic of Prayer in Learning* (Cardiff: University of Wales Press, 2012), this new book builds on the concepts of ministerial and priestly formation explored there; but it can be read on its own.

A key theme in ministerial formation concerns the identity and role of the minister. This can be approached through important functionalist questions: What really is the job of the Christian priest or leader? What is expected of me and what skills will I need? Or the issue of identity can be explored through more significant ontological questions: What am I becoming? What happens when the raw material of my life and my gifting encounters the role of priest? In what sense might this calling be a *sign* to others of the type of kingdom we believe in? This book will resource all kinds of contemporary questioning about the role of priest or leader and bring a fresh angle to the mysterious process of ministerial formation. Existing manuals on Christian leadership seem eminently sensible. They speak of forming strategy, leading teams, handling conflict – all in a biblical way, of course.[11] This book aims to be different – not because of novelty but because of the unending freshness of New Testament Christology and the experience of clergy in today's risky post-modern world.

Aim of this book

So in this book I want to do two things. First, I want to unearth these images of Jesus that will both unsettle and inspire ministry today – images that emerge from research in the Holy Land about the first century and that resonate strongly with the practice of ministry today. They will turn out, I think, to be authentically ancient and refreshingly contemporary. They speak powerfully about leadership in a way both unnerving and enlivening. I hope they will be a catalyst and stimulus to all involved in ministry, whether as priests, deacons, leaders or lay assistants. Second, as we explore the enigma of Jesus through these images, we discover how they inform not only the practice of Christian leadership today but also a leader's spirituality – whether you want to call it priestly spirituality or the spirituality of leadership.

Prayer exercises at the end of each chapter indicate how we might pray our way with these images today. Most chapters follow a similar pattern. First we examine the model of Jesus, noting the scholarship and examining the evidence. Then we start to see what this suggests to our practice of ministry. A set of penetrating questions is offered, for individual reflection or group use, together with ideas for further reading.

Readership and use

The Archbishop of Canterbury has recently reminded us that one of the priorities for the Church at this time is to 're-imagine ministry'.[12] This book is intended to help us on that process and journey. It is for all concerned with ministry and leadership. It is intended to inspire clergy – especially those looking for a fresh view of the priesthood or diaconate today. It is for those exploring a vocation to ordained ministry. It is also for lay leaders and all involved in ministry today, in all its many forms. The book is also offered to our brothers and sisters in the free churches and house churches as they evolve patterns of ministry appropriate to the new century. In short – it is hoped that the book will unsettle, disturb, hearten and inspire.

The cover, bearing a representation of the sixth-century icon of 'Christ of Sinai', sums up this book. The two eyes of Christ are quite different – his right eye is clear and penetrating in its gaze, while his left eye is tear-filled and compassionate. As the icon encapsulates the mystery and paradox of Jesus of Nazareth, so this book explores contrasting dimensions of Christ that cast fresh light on our ministry and mission today.

1

Jesus the builder

Creativity and courage in ministry

———◆•◆•◆———

A raw, sinewy, visceral image presents itself. Jesus, as a young man, dripping in sweat beneath the midday sun, heaving heavy rocks in his strong arms. Jesus, hammer in hand, chipping away at massive pieces of stone, shaping them for use in a great edifice. Jesus, working on a construction site, becoming alert to the exploitation and oppression of workers. This is the Jesus we are rediscovering – Jesus the builder and craftsman.

In the past the Greek word *tecton*, used to describe Jesus' occupation, has been translated 'carpenter' (Mark 6.3; Matt. 13.55). We have been brought up with images of Jesus working as an apprentice in his father's workshop in Nazareth, perhaps even thinking of the cross as he shapes wood. But scholars now tell us the word can be translated 'builder' or 'worker in stone', 'mason', even 'contractor' or 'engineer'. Recent archaeology has revealed that very close to Nazareth, at the time Jesus was in his teens and twenties, there was a building site of extraordinary scale. In the 1990s and continuing into the new century, excavation teams from Duke University and the Hebrew University of Jerusalem have made some astonishing discoveries about the city of Sepphoris (Zippori), about an hour's walk from Nazareth. It offered unparalleled opportunities for a *tecton*, and it is more than likely that Jesus worked there regularly. Nazareth itself, being a village of only 200 souls, offered very limited opportunities for work, while Sepphoris was calling out for craftsmen. What was going on at Sepphoris?

The former town had been destroyed in 4 BC in a brutal crushing of a Jewish uprising soon after the death of Herod the Great. The Roman army, led by Varus, burned the city and emptied it.

1

But Herod Antipas, son of Herod the Great, had plans for its resurrection. Indeed, Josephus tells us, he wanted it to rise from the ashes as a brand new regional capital, the jewel or ornament of all Galilee. And so it experienced a rebirth precisely at the time Jesus was working as a *tecton* just four miles away in Nazareth. It re-established itself as an opulent Hellenized town for a Greek/ Jewish aristocracy. It may indeed be the 'city built on a hill' that 'cannot be hidden' (Matt. 5.14).

In one sense it was an exciting construction site, with different contractors building roads, new villas and great public buildings, such as a synagogue and theatre.[1] Jesus would have applied his versatile skills as an artisan. On the woodworking side he made and installed scaffolding, preparing wooden beams for the ceiling, shaping window frames and doors. In stone, Jesus chiselled at the limestone blocks and released the designs hidden within them. He shaped and reshaped the stones so they would fit together within arches and be able to welcome the keystone or cornerstone of the vault. Such work took a trained eye and strong physical exertion; it required both patience and precision.

Lessons from the building site

What lessons did Jesus learn from the building site? In these formative years he became exposed to cruel inequality and oppressions. He would ask himself at whose expense these constructions were being made. The Galilee region of Jesus' time was a place of increasing poverty, witnessing ever more polarization between rich and poor. An exploitative and grasping urban elite resided in the affluent cities of Tiberias and Sefforis, while in their humble lakeside villages Jewish peasants barely eked out a living.

At Sefforis Jesus learns to listen to his fellow workers and hears of their heartaches and pain and debt. Soon, when the time is ripe, he will travel throughout the region with a radical message about the kingdom of God where all are equal and valued. There is no doubt Jesus became increasingly uncomfortable and disturbed by what he saw – and this clarified and crystallized his very message about the kingdom, about the possibility of a different way of living, that we will explore in Chapter 3, 'Jesus the rebel'. Such parables as the expendable day workers (Matt. 20.1–15) proclaimed the valuing of every worker. Within God's kingdom there will be a place for all – unlike Sepphoris, which spoke so painfully of the apartheid of the 'haves' and 'have nots'.[2]

Building metaphors in Jesus' teaching

In the Hebrew Scriptures the prophet Isaiah had depicted God as a builder in relation to his people: 'For as a young man marries a young woman, so shall your builder marry you, and as the bridegroom rejoices over the bride, so shall your God rejoice over you' (Isa. 62.5). It is significant that in his teaching ministry, Jesus rarely refers in his parables to wood or trees, as a carpenter might, but made repeated references to building with rock.[3]

His experience at Sepphoris gave him a vivid range of metaphors: 'Everyone then who hears these words of mine and acts on them will be like a wise man who built his house on rock' (Matt. 7.24). Undoubtedly, his firsthand experience on the construction site of Sepphoris gave him insight into building ambitions and human avarice: 'Listen to another parable. There was a landowner who planted a vineyard, put a fence around it, dug a wine press in it, and built a watch-tower' (Matt. 21.33; Mark 11.27). 'Then he [the rich man] said, "I will do this: I will pull down my barns and build larger ones, and there I will store all my grain and my goods"' (Luke 12.18).

From the building site Jesus was able to see lessons that applied to the cost of discipleship:

> For which of you, intending to build a tower, does not first sit down and estimate the cost . . . Otherwise . . . all who see it will begin to ridicule him saying 'This fellow began to build and was not able to finish.'   (Luke 14.28–30)

The vocation of Jesus

In more than one sense Jesus recognized in the image of the builder or construction worker a glimpse of his own vocation.

God was calling him to build something new, beautiful and in-destructible, his *ecclesia*: 'And I tell you, you are Peter, and on this rock I will build my church, and the gates of Hades will not pre-vail against it' (Matt. 16.18). However, it was in Jerusalem that Jesus saw his vocation, more clearly than ever before, in terms of both demolition and rebuilding.

> As he came out of the temple, one of his disciples said to him, 'Look, Teacher, what large stones and what large buildings!' Then Jesus said to him, 'Do you see these great buildings? Not one stone will be left here upon another; all will be thrown down.' (Mark 13.1–2)

The massive structure of the temple, limestone glistening in the bright Jerusalem sunlight, had only recently been completed. Herod the Great had undertaken a massive building project: the construc-tion of a vast platform atop Mount Zion, with retaining walls still to be seen today – the Western or Wailing Wall – made of impressive dressed stones, many weighing over five tons. All were overwhelmed by the beauty of the new temple, and its seeming permanence. However, looking at the temple Jesus realized pre-cisely what God was calling him to. He knew the Scriptures: the call of the Jerusalem prophet Jeremiah, with whom he closely identified:[4] 'I appoint you over nations and over kingdoms, to pluck up and to pull down, to destroy and to overthrow, to build and to plant' (Jer. 1.10). Jesus knew the words of Ecclesiastes: there is 'a time to break down, and a time to build up' (3.3). And so standing within the temple precincts, Jesus says: 'Destroy this temple, and in three days I will raise it up'. There was an outcry: 'The Jews then said, "This temple has been under construction for forty-six years, and will you raise it up in three days?"' (John 2.19–20).

John adds: 'But he was speaking of the temple of his body' (v. 21). It is probable that we are getting close here to what Jesus really thought about the meaning of his own vocation, his death and his resurrection. The accusation that he made a claim to destroy and rebuild the temple appears, unusually, in all four Gospels and so may well go back to an authentic utterance of Jesus, albeit symbolic and cryptic. Moreover there is a consensus among scholars that the event we label 'the cleansing of the temple' (the overturning of tables and their crashing to the ground) is best understood as a prophetic action by Jesus bespeaking the very destruction of the temple – no mere clearout, but its very ending.[5] Jesus, it seems, had a stunningly outrageous understanding of his calling and identity. He was to be the new locus of the divine! Since 970 BC the divine had been thought to reside in the temple, represented there, first of all, by the Ark of the Covenant placed in the Holy of Holies. 'See, something greater than Solomon is here' (Matt. 12.42). Jesus is pointing to himself, to his very body, as the place where God is now to be discovered. But this is no painless theophany: there is to be a violent desecration and destruction of the temple of his body, and it is to be laid in ruins, before something new and mysterious is to arise.

Killed in a quarry

It is significant that Jesus is killed in a quarry.[6] The rock of Calvary itself may have been left standing amid the ancient quarry outside the city wall precisely because it was useless – a deep fracture running from its top into the earth indicates that it was unsuitable for use in building – it became a rejected rock. The first Christians, seeking to make sense of the event of Calvary, turned to the Hebrew Scriptures and there found texts that spoke of a rejected rock being used in God's rebuilding purposes for humanity: 'The stone that the builders rejected has become the chief cornerstone' (Ps. 118.22). This verse is used by different communities in the New Testament and is quoted in Mark, Matthew, Luke in the Holy Week story, by Peter in his sermon in Acts 4 and by the writer of 1 Peter 2.7. Jesus is also understood as 'a stone one strikes against . . . a rock one stumbles over' (Isa. 8.14). But such a stone becomes the keystone in the new work, the new temple that God is building, for a further text from Isaiah inspired the first Christians: 'See, I am laying in Zion a foundation stone, a tested stone, a precious cornerstone, a sure foundation' (28.16). This is quoted in Romans (9.33) and 1 Peter (2.4–6). The rock of Golgotha, standing to this day, is at once a memorial to the crucifixion and a pointer to a new future.

Today the rock of Calvary is part of a complex in the Church of the Holy Sepulchre that makes up 'the rock of our salvation'.[7] The empty cave of Christ's tomb, which Constantine had separated from the surrounding rock, is the timeless witness, the testimony to the reality of Christ's victory: 'The venerable and most holy memorial [*martyrion*] of the Saviour's resurrection', as Eusebius called it. In front of the rock of Calvary and the empty tomb, Constantine constructed a spectacular basilica, which became the focus of Christian pilgrimage for centuries. This very building became a testament in stone to the resurrection of Christ – the stone that the builders rejected truly became the cornerstone!

Ministerial formation: God's creativity in us

Ministerial formation attests to God's ever-creative process of shaping our lives, God's awesome creativity. Indeed, the language of formation evokes the accounts of creation: 'the LORD God formed man from the dust of the ground, and breathed into his nostrils the breath of life; and the man became a living being' (Gen. 2.7). It recalls the language of the psalms. Psalm 139.13–15 wonders at God's secret moulding of the person in the womb. Psalm 33.15 talks about God forming the inner person: 'he who fashions the hearts of them all'. Jeremiah's image of the potter working on the clay (18.1–6) reminds us that God not only makes us of dust of the earth but wants to shape us. God can do wonderful things with the 'raw material' of a human life yielded to his hands. The song puts it: 'Spirit of the living God, fall afresh on me . . . break me, melt me, mould me, fill me.' Formation is a process by which a person gets reshaped. 'Do not remember the former things, or consider the things of old. I am about to do a new thing; now it springs forth, do you not perceive it?' (Isa. 43.18–19).

Key New Testament passages

What does the New Testament suggest should be our priorities in working with God as co-builders and co-workers? Various New Testament writers explore the pastoral and leadership dimensions of the powerful building and formation metaphor, and there are three key passages to be pondered, throwing up some tough questions.

Develop resources

> According to the grace of God given to me, like a skilled master builder I laid a foundation, and someone else is building on it. Each builder must choose with care how to build on it ... Do you not know that you are God's temple and that God's Spirit dwells in you?   (1 Cor. 3.10, 16)

Read the whole passage (1 Cor. 3.10–17). Paul calls himself 'a skilled master builder'.

- What skills do you think he displayed in building Christian community?
- What building skills do you seek to develop in your ministry?
- How do you show that you value and appreciate all the materials and resources available in your community?

Build a temple

> In him [Christ Jesus] the whole structure is joined together and grows into a holy temple in the Lord; in whom you also are built together spiritually into a dwelling-place for God.
> (Eph. 2.21–22)

Read the whole passage (Eph. 2.19–22). We trace the idea of God's temple reaching fulfilment in the body of Jesus and in the body of Christ, the Church.

- How does seeing the people of your congregation in terms of a sanctuary and dwelling place of God affect your ministry to them?

Get ready to be reshaped

> Come to him, a living stone, though rejected by mortals yet
> chosen and precious in God's sight, and like living stones, let
> yourselves be built into a spiritual house.   (1 Peter 2.4–5)

Read the whole passage (1 Peter 2.4–9). Stones need to be 'dressed'
or reshaped with chisel and hammer before they can be used – this
is essential so that they fit together properly in the structure under
construction.

- In what ways have you experienced your own ministerial
  formation – and Christian formation among 'living stones' –
  as a painful process?

The living stone is 'rejected by mortals' and the temple of Christ's
body is to be torn down (John 2.19).

- How central to ministry and leadership do you see the place
  of sacrifice?
- In what ways do you expect priesthood or ministry to be a
  costly business?

Recall Luke 14.28–29.

- Looking again at this reading, what issues in Christian formation
  do you stumble over?

One of my present jobs is being parish priest to one of England's
earliest church buildings, seventh-century St Andrew's church at
Bishopstone in East Sussex. The building has stood here for more
than 1,300 years. It is essentially a Saxon structure, built mainly
from rubble! In my mind's eye I picture the parishioners, labourers
and farmworkers collecting, over several years, flint stones from
the local fields as they are ploughed up – these small rocks will
form lasting walls several feet thick! These walls have withstood
pirate raids from across the Channel and the fiercest storms. The
plan is modest but robust. I see important lessons in this construction. First, such modest stones are not to be despised – substantial
structures can be built from humble resources. Second, the
construction of the church depended on team building and the

involvement of many people, of all ages and abilities, in the village. Third, the church took years to be built, from the gathering of the resources to the noble, finished Saxon nave. The people were patient and determined, could see the potential of a church in a pile of rocks gathered from the farm. A simple but clear plan shaped up in their mind and came to fruition through a process of prayer and work, perseverance and resolve.

Questions for reflection

1 What are you aiming at, as priest or pastor or leader? What are your plans? What do you hope will be your lasting legacy? Recall Hebrews 11.10: Abraham 'looked forward to the city that has foundations, whose architect and builder is God'. Recall too Psalm 127.1: 'Unless the LORD builds the house, those who build it labour in vain.'
2 In what ways does your church resemble a construction site?
3 Are there things that need to be torn down before something new emerges? As in Sefforis and Jerusalem, is there a work of demolition to be accomplished before renewal comes?
4 What is truly the foundation of your ministry?
5 What else are you learning from the image of Jesus as artist, craftsman and builder?

Prayer exercise

Take a stone and hold it in the palm of your hand. Take a close look at it and admire its uniqueness. Are there rough or smooth parts to it? There is only one just like this, with its particular markings and structure. Make friends with it!

Its *past*: Where has this stone come from? What is its past, its history? What great cliff or mountain was it once part of? What is its geological story? Wonder about what happened to this rock. Was it pounded by waves in the sea? Was it polished by the movement of ice?

Its *future*: What will become of this stone? Will it be taken by a youth and thrown through a window? Just lie unwanted on the ground? Will this stone be used in a structure – a wall, an art installation? Will it be carefully reshaped and remoulded by an artist or mason?

Finally, let this stone speak to you of your own life, past and future. You have a unique history and your own special gifting. Give thanks to God for his providence and provision. Thank God for your own 'markings' – those things about yourself, your appearance and personality, that make you different.

As you hold the stone in your hands, realize that God holds you lovingly in his hands. And he has plans for you. Like a mason, like a *tecton*, he desires to shape and reshape your life – to mould you into his image, to use you in the great building work of his kingdom. As Peter put it: 'like living stones, let yourselves be built into a spiritual house' (1 Pet. 2.5). Rejoice that your life is raw material in the hands of the creator and redeemer God. Give thanks that he has an unfolding design and purpose for your unique life. Entrust yourself afresh to God, remembering: 'We are God's work of art' (Eph. 2.10, Jerusalem Bible).

Further reading

R. A. Batey, *Jesus and the Forgotten City: New Light on Sepphoris and the Urban World of Jesus* (Grand Rapids, MI: Baker Book House, 1991).

J. D. Crossan and J. L. Reed, *Excavating Jesus* (London: SPCK, 2001).

D. J. Tidball, *Builders and Fools: Leadership the Bible Way* (Leicester: Inter-Varsity Press, 1999).

2

Jesus the hermit

Energizing solitude in ministry

———•◦•———

Jesus, a hermit? We think of him as gregarious, reaching out to others in healing and teaching, always surrounded by crowds, by the multitudes. But a closer reading of the Gospels not only reveals a strong hermit-character in Jesus but also points us towards understanding the very secret of his leadership.

Jesus was *literally* a hermit, for the word derives from the Greek word *eremos*, which features strongly in the Gospel accounts: it means 'lonely or deserted place'. Mentioned many times in the narratives, it denotes the experience of aloneness, solitude that Jesus craved for. We shall look at how the Gospels use this word to describe a place or state so favoured by Jesus. Jesus was, second, *literally* an anchorite, a solitary: the word derives from the verb that keeps cropping up in the accounts: *anachoreo*, 'to withdraw', 'to make retreat', 'to retire'. These two hermit-words became basic to the earliest monastic vocabulary – a grammar or language of solitude – describing the early monastic experience of detachment from the world.

Basil of Caesarea (330–79), for example, finds these terms central to the monastic experience. After researching the first monastic settlements of Palestine, Syria and Egypt, on his return to Cappadocia he embodied his insights in his *Rule*, which to this day is central to Eastern monasticism.[1] In his letter to his friend Gregory Nazianzus, written to persuade him to come and join the retreat at Pontus, Basil explores these two aspects of the call of the desert.[2]

Basil explains: 'The solitude [*eremia*] offers a very great advantage for our task of prayer. Let us for a season be free from the

11

commerce of men, so that nothing may come from without and break the continuity of the training.' Second, the desert calls us to detachment: 'Now this withdrawal [*anachoresis*, retreat] does not mean that we should leave the world bodily, but rather break loose from the ties of "sympathy" of the soul with the body.' Basil extols the virtues of making a retreat from activity, for a few minutes, hours or days. He says that, for a season, we have to cut our ties, loosen our grip and grasp on activities, let go of our attachments and worries so we can become wholly available to God in prayer.

This is precisely what we see happening in the experience of Jesus. It is not possible, of course, to reconstruct from the Gospels Jesus' interior life or his psychology, but we get glimpses, pointers, indicators to this. We can certainly examine the role the evangelists give to Jesus retreating to a place of isolation and seclusion and how this functions in the narrative; we can notice the part played by the *eremos* in the context of the Gospel story, by the *anachoresis*, noting what came before – what triggered the retreat – and how Jesus behaves afterwards. This will give us some clues as to the effect of the silence on Jesus, at least in the eyes of the Gospel writers. We will be attentive to how at particular moments the evangelists deliberately employ the significant and more highly charged verb *anachoreo*, denoting 'to make a retreat' instead of the more common verbs 'to go', *ágo* or *ápeimi*.

Moreover we shall discover that the hermit life is key to Jesus' survival in ministry, humanly speaking, and the very well-spring of his inspiration. It will not be difficult for us to draw lessons for our own practice of leadership. Recently I have had the privilege of interviewing a number of newly ordained clergy, together with their tutors in theological college or course, for a piece of doctoral research on ministerial formation. Extracts from some of these conversations will be appended below and will illustrate how the aspects of Jesus' solitary prayer resonate with contemporary experience.[3] As we look at the Gospels we see solitude functioning in at least five ways in the ministry of Jesus.

Clarifying vocation

Three scenes stand out: the desert, the mountain and the garden. Jesus begins his ministry in the wilderness. After his baptism he is driven by the Spirit into the inner desert. He discovers it to be a place of angels and demons, or as Mark puts it succinctly: 'He was in the wilderness forty days, tempted by Satan; and he was with the wild beasts; and the angels waited on him' (Mark 1.13). Jesus experienced the desert as a place of conflict, in which he decisively battled with shortcuts to prestige and power. But here, most of all, he learned to discern the Father's voice, and discovered the priorities for his ensuing ministry. Here he discovered what was to become the secret of his ministry: 'Very truly, I tell you, the Son can do nothing on his own, but only what he sees the Father doing . . . The Father loves the Son and shows him all that he himself is doing' (John 5.19–20). In his desert prayer Jesus glimpses the divine imperatives that will guide him in the days ahead.

It is in the desert that Jesus clarifies his priorities and his over-arching vision. Like the very landscape, he lays bare his soul to God. As the wind blows over the desert so the Spirit, who drove him into the wilderness, breezes into his soul and energizes him for what is to come.

In leadership terms we would say that Jesus ponders and sets his strategy in his desert prayer. We see this pattern recurring in his ministry, for at crucial moments he enters the hermit state. Before Jesus makes the major decision about those he will call to be the core of the new people of God, fulfilling the twelve tribes of Israel, he devotes long hours of prayer, in the darkness of the night: 'Now during those days he went out to the mountain to pray; and he spent the night in prayer to God. And when day came, he called his disciples and chose twelve of them, whom he also named apostles' (Luke 6.12–13).

Jesus clarifies his vocation in the context of solitude and prayer in the Transfiguration. Luke tells us the reason for Jesus' ascent of the mountain: he went up the mountain to pray. He had reached a crossroads in his ministry, a watershed: at Caesarea Philippi he had asked his disciples to declare their understanding of him, and he began to speak, for the first time, of his coming passion in Jerusalem. While Peter could not handle the idea of a suffering messiah, Jesus spoke of the passion of the Son of Man. Now, on the holy mountain, Jesus mystically engages with two displaced persons: Moses and Elijah. Moses speaks with him about the exodus Jesus is to accomplish in Jerusalem. Truly this prayer experience clarifies to Jesus his vocation more strongly than ever. Now he can see very clearly what he has to do. We might use the word 'discernment' in relation to what is going on in the hermit prayer of Jesus.

The theme of vocation resurfaces in Jesus' prayer in Gethsemane. On the night of his passion Jesus goes directly from the room of the Last Supper to a favourite place of retreat. Luke tells us it was his custom to make retreat in the garden of Gethsemane, at the foot of the Mount of Olives, a secluded spot across the Kidron valley from the temple. There in the darkness Jesus ponders his fate and considers different options represented in sword and chalice. He moves from resistance and hesitation to a place of surrender as he embraces his destiny. In his prayer he discovers fresh reserves of courage.

One of the young clergy experienced this discernment in these terms:

> Actually it's something about not taking God to people but helping them to discover that he's already there, and I think in some ways that links quite strongly in with prayer. It involves getting involved but also being able to take a step back and *actually* trying to be aware of where God is at work and praying for those people there. It's discerning where God is at work, where you are called to be at a certain time and in some ways waiting on that developing . . . but a lot of it is about making connections, trying to find out where we are called to be, rather than where we think we might be called to be or where we would necessarily like to be. And that does come back, in various different ways, to prayer. (*a*)[4]

Healing grief

We see Jesus entering solitude after two momentous events involving the fate of John the Baptist, his arrest and his death. First we see in Matthew 4.12: 'Now when Jesus heard that John had been arrested, he withdrew [*anechoreesen*] to Galilee.' In the perspective of the first evangelist, Jesus receives news that John his cousin has been jailed. He is stunned by the news and goes into solitude to gain some perspective on the situation. What does it mean for him and his timing? He realizes that with the removal of his forerunner and precursor from the scene, now is the time to begin his public ministry in earnest. Jesus had, it seems, lingered in the lower Jordan valley after his time in the Judean desert. The news of John's captivity causes him to head north. As Mark puts it: 'Now after John was arrested, Jesus came to Galilee, proclaiming the good news of God, and saying, "The time is fulfilled, and the kingdom of God has come near; repent, and believe in the good news"' (Mark 1.14–15). For Jesus, *chronos* turns to *kairos*. There are two ways of looking at time: *chronos* denotes successive events of history, coming one after another in a linear fashion, but *kairos* denotes God's time, God's inbreaking into history, the hour of opportunity, the moment of grace. Mark tells us that Jesus greets this event as a *kairos* moment – the time has come, the hour has dawned, God's reign is imminent and within reach! But, Matthew tells us, Jesus gains this revelation of God's timing through his *anachoresis*, his withdrawal, his retreat. The retreat affords an opportunity to process the pain of the news and to see John's arrest not as a tragedy but as an opportunity; not as a disaster but as a disclosure – of God's unfolding will and purposes.

We see this, second, when the news of John's death reaches Jesus' ears. He learns the sorry tale of how the daughter of Herodias acquired the head of John the Baptist on a platter at a public dinner party. What is his reaction? Matthew tells us: 'Now when Jesus heard this, he withdrew [*anechoreesen*] from there in a boat to a deserted place [*eremos*] by himself' (14.13). The account is triply emphatic of solitude: Jesus withdrew, made a retreat; to an *eremos* ('lonely place'); by himself, in his own company. He needs a space alone. He needs to process his grief and heartbreak. As he thinks of John's violent demise, he no doubt ponders his own fate and destiny. Will this be his path as well? In the silence of

15

his retreat he faces not only his sorrow but also his fears and forebodings. Is this what lies in store for him, and how soon?

But this time of aloneness also renews and re-equips Jesus, in Matthew's perspective. He emerges from this desert experience to reveal what Matthew (14.14) calls 'compassion'. The Greek word communicates an intensity: it denotes being moved with tenderness or pity in one's inward parts. Of course, in English the word has the connotation 'to suffer with' someone. Jesus has found his silence transformative. He begins with mourning mingled with fear but ends with a heart brimming over with strong love and compassion for the crowds, a deep empathy and solidarity with those who are facing illness, vulnerability and fragility in their human compassion. Jesus' grief does not lead to self-pity – 'Am I next?' – but to solidarity with those who suffer. And he immediately recognizes the leadership gap – for, Matthew tells us, they were 'like sheep without a shepherd' (9.36). After his withdrawal, Jesus is ready to advance. He has discovered the re-energizing effects of silence.

Several clergy right across the spectrum of age and tradition spoke of 'unloading' the day's pressures through prayer, and recognized its therapeutic effects in healing pain and grief. An evangelical in her forties gave a candid account:

> Sometimes life and ministry can be frenetic – and after a difficult pastoral situation or difficult visit, extempore prayer would help me offer it to God, or someone praying with me. Especially after an emotional situation, a tough situation, I need to unload it onto God . . . And I bring to God too my frustrations from things in the parish. Prayer helps me make some sense of parish life and its demands . . . I need to share with God on a regular basis or I couldn't do it. I think prayer gives me hope. Prayer is the thing that sustains me, and prayer gives me the whole meaning of my life. Prayer is my lifeline – it keeps me sane. The silence rejuvenates my spirit. (*g*)

Thus prayer can enable the release of pent-up emotions, and the expression of anger when necessary. Several clergy valued the Psalms in particular as a way to bring frustrations and questions to God in prayer in an acceptable and time-honoured way: 'Like the psalmist, you can have a good rant and rave but end up blessing God' (*d*). Two spoke of tears in prayer: 'a real release of something I wasn't conscious of' (*c*). One spoke in terms of becoming in prayer 'enfolded in God's love, feeling his presence, feeling safe' (*b*).

Handling conflict

Matthew's Gospel emphasizes Jesus' struggle with the Pharisees – his original readership was separating from the synagogue. Matthew states more than once that Jesus makes a retreat after an intense time of confrontation, controversy and argument with the Jewish religious experts on the law. An experience of conflict leads directly to a time of silence in which Jesus regains his perspective. His argument with the Pharisees over healing on the sabbath culminates in a death threat: 'the Pharisees went out and conspired against him, how to destroy him.' The account immediately goes on: 'Jesus, aware of this, withdrew [*anechoreesen*] from there' (12.14–15, ESV). His collision with enemies leads to withdrawal, to a space in which, somewhat battered and bruised, he both regains composure and discovers new energy for the next round of the fight, which ensues immediately (12.22–37). Jesus is able to take on the Pharisees with a renewed authority, which springs from his time of silence. He speaks with fresh gravitas: 'Every kingdom divided against itself is laid waste . . . if it is by the Spirit of God that I cast out demons, then the kingdom of God has come to you' (12.25, 28).

John's Gospel too depicts Jesus making a retreat after a significant moment of potential contention: 'When Jesus realized that they were about to come and take him by force to make him king, he withdrew [*anechoreesen*] again to the mountain by himself' (John 6.15). Now it is the fourth evangelist's time to employ this key verb. This is a highly poignant challenge to which Jesus chooses to respond by making a retreat, because it concerns the heart of his vocation. The people want Jesus to be a political messiah, leading deliverance from the Roman occupiers. They want a king. But Jesus will not take this path, and decisively turns his back on this option. The withdrawal gives him a chance to take stock, refocus and reorientate himself after this perhaps scary approach – 'by force' – from the crowd. He makes an *anachoresis* not only to protect himself from this row and affray but to regain perspective on his true calling: to be not a political king but bread to be shared for the world (John 6.16ff.).

Matthew gives other examples of how conflict leads to a period of withdrawal. Jerusalem scribes and Pharisees enter into bitter contention with Jesus over the issue of external washings and ablutions (Matt. 15). Jesus will not tolerate this ritual drained of morality and states that it is the heart that matters (15.18–19). After this further bout in the ongoing combat the evangelist tells us: 'Jesus went away from there and withdrew [*anechoreesen*] to the district of Tyre and Sidon' (15.21, RSV). Jesus makes a journey across the northern mountains of Galilee to a retreat location on the coast where he knows he will be able to introduce the disciples to different cultures and world views: there he meets the Syro-phoenician woman, who will challenge him over the big issue of who is welcome in God's kingdom. After this set-to and clash with the woman, Jesus makes his way up into the hills above Galilee and there he 'sat down' (15.29). Surely he is ready for another rest – but he doesn't get it!

A tutor, training a new generation of Christian leaders, celebrates the healing aspect of prayer:

> When you're faced with the world you get bogged down with it, you allow yourself to be dissipated – and then you come together again; you are drawn into one, you are integrated, reintegrated, by finding once again the source of all being. And so, in a sense, the movement into contemplation feels like a movement away from concerns. But there is a way in which you have to let it all go and let it into the mind and heart of God, in order to pick it up again with one's own mind changed, so that when you go back into the cycle of mission, you are renewed. (*m*)

Renewing focus

Both Mark and Luke emphasize the role of prayer and silence in the example Jesus sets before the disciples, following the 40 days of prayer, struggle and preparation in the desert. In Mark 1 a hectic 24 hours of ministry is followed by prayer before dawn in an *eremos* – 'lonely place' (1.35). The time of prayer is both the conclusion of an intense period of ministry and the prelude to the next stage. This rhythm of prayer and activity is repeated in the disciples' experience: after first incursions into ministry they give an account of their experience to Jesus and he responds: 'Come away to a deserted place [*eremos*] all by yourselves and rest a while' (Mark 6.30–31). William Lane points out: 'In each instance reference to the wilderness-place is preceded by an account of Jesus' preaching and power; he then withdraws from the multitude which seeks his gifts.'[5] After this retreat another time of ministry (6.35–45) is followed by Christ's retirement into the hills for prayer at night (6.46) – the pattern of intense activity and solitude is repeated.

The interviews revealed that clergy face many kinds of stress in the parish that threaten the identity and confidence of the minister. Some feel battered and bruised, if not hurt by ministry:

I think the busier things get, in a way, the more you need to stop and have time for prayer . . . I think I did spend the first few months running around like a headless chicken and in many ways did feel I'd lost direction in terms of why I was doing it. Now I see it: the more you have practically to do, the more important it is to make sure that you're rooted in prayer, that prayer becomes a priority, rather than the thing that gets squeezed out. If you don't make sure that you're always keeping God at the core then it's very easy to begin valuing things for their own sake. That is especially dangerous in this job because there are so many facets to it – I suspect it's probably quite easy to let prayer (and therefore God) get squeezed out and lose the reason why you're doing things . . . It's a fragmented job in many ways but it all stems from one thing and it's actually remembering that it all comes back to that one thing that is the important aspect. I think prayer helps you to put things in the true perspective that they're supposed to be in. I mean, you can get sucked into so many day-to-day things ... hundreds of things to worry about, and it can seem very fragmented, but it's actually a case of thinking, well, it is all part of a larger picture, of a wider picture, and that is God, really ... it's for me to learn to be open to discerning God's will and hearing God's call. If all the fragmented strands of life are gathered up in an individual and corporate relationship with God, then things have a habit of turning out to be less fragmented and strange than they otherwise appear! (*a*)

Prayer, especially types that enable reflective space, can function as survival techniques for hard-pressed clergy.

Sometimes I come to prayer feeling quite flustered – the busy-ness of life again – and praying helps me to take my foot off the pedal a bit, just to relax, and hand things over to God, recognize that it's not just me doing this. Prayer helps me hugely with the demands and stresses of ministry – I think it's vital. I'm aware that when prayer gets squeezed out then, in myself, I'm not operating in a right sort of way, in a spiritual sort of way. I can slip into a worldly way of doing things, which is just about being busy and getting jobs done and ticking things off the list. So prayer is absolutely vital in that process of reorientating yourself. (*e*)

Hermit-like prayer enables a process of making sense of ministry. One tutor puts it eloquently:

I think that without returning to the centre of things, without returning to the source of all life, we will simply run out of steam, get choked up with all sorts of good ideas and never know which one is the best idea, and there will probably be a dissociation of roles, where we can no longer say who we are. The thing about prayer is that it has to be an activity of the heart, and the heart is the centre of our being ... So prayer of whatever type, has to be the centre if we want to stay in one piece. (*m*)

Learning deeply

Luke links prayer and deep learning. In three events Jesus' prayer time looks like the seedbed of his teaching and the place of his theological reflection, because the silence is broken by Jesus speaking words of instruction. In Luke 6 Jesus withdraws to the hills and prays through the night after a demanding period in which great crowds gathered for preaching and healing (Luke 6.12). This prayer time leads directly to the Sermon on the Plain (6.20ff.), suggesting that the Beatitudes and Woes took shape during his night of prayer. We see a second example in Luke 9. After another period of intense ministry a further time of prayer becomes the context for learning and questions: 'Once when Jesus was praying alone, with only the disciples near him, he asked them, "Who do the crowds say that I am?"' (9.18). After prayer, Jesus teaches about the suffering Son of Man (9.22).

A third example of the relationship between prayer and learning is found as Christ spontaneously moves into a prayer of thanksgiving after the disciples' period of debriefing and theological reflection shared on their return from ministry (Luke 10). Jesus gives thanks for the gift of revelation – *apokalupsis* – taking place in the pastoral experience of the Seventy (Luke 10.21).

As James Dunn puts it, we should note 'the degree to which Jesus provided a model to his disciples as a man of prayer ... To be a disciple of Jesus was to pray as Jesus prayed.'[6] Christ's exemplifying a balance between prayer and activity is communicated not only by his own personal practice but by appeal to other expressions, notably in the passage about Mary and Martha in which Mary chooses 'the better part' (Luke 10.38–42). Jesus then models praying himself and this leads directly into teaching (Luke 11.1). He speaks of the kind of prayer that involves bringing questions and puzzlement to God: 'Ask, and it will be given to you; search, and you will find; knock and the door will be opened for you' (Luke 11.9).

This resonates with what educationists are saying about 'deep learning'. Guy Claxton distinguishes between two modes of learning: 'd-mode' mental activity, involved in rational, conscious and intellectual thinking, and slow ways of knowing, the more non-rational, less linear processes of what he calls the 'undermind'. He argues that Western educational practice favours the 'd-mode' activity and that the use of the 'undermind' should be nurtured: 'D-mode must be developed and refined, but so must be the powers of intuition and imagination, of careful, non-verbal observation, of listening to the body, of detecting (without harvesting them too quickly) small seeds of insight.'[7]

A recurring theme in the interviews is that prayer, especially the reflective type, enables a different way of looking at reality and is inseparable from theological reflection.

> Theological reflection becomes a way of approaching things and a way of looking at things and interpreting things, which is actually, I would say, almost a way of prayer. It's trying to look for where God is in this and be open to where God is in that, rather than trying to *apply* God to a particular situation. Prayer and theological reflection are in many ways one and the same – it's the eyes through which you look at things. (*a*)

Withdrawal – and return

Jesus does not stay a hermit or anchorite. He brings his stillness into the midst of the noisy world: his desert heart still pulsates within him. But he must leave the lonely places – heartened, challenged, instructed, comforted and energized – to face the demands of ministry and the call of the cross. This rhythm between withdrawal and engagement, this ebb and flow of prayer and ministry, is the key to the ministry of Jesus: we noted that, in John's view, he only does what he hears the Father telling him, in his listening prayer (John 5.19–20; 14.10). On the mount of transfiguration Peter wants to build three booths to give Jesus and his companions a place in which they can dwell. He wants to hold on to the moment. Jesus will have none of that. He leads the disciples down the mountain right into the place of desperate human need. We go with him, echoing the hymn by Armitage Robinson:

> 'Tis good, Lord, to be here,
> Yet we may not remain;
> but since thou bidst us leave the mount,
> come with us to the plain.

Questions for reflection

1 What difference do you think the experience of solitude made to Jesus' ministry?
2 Which of the five ways that solitude enhanced Jesus' ministry resonate with your experience?
3 Why are we fearful of solitude? Why is the word 'hermit' regarded sometimes as unattractive or eccentric?
4 Why is the hermit experience crucial to leadership?
5 What steps can you take to incorporate solitude into your practice of ministry?

Prayer exercise

Choose a 'lonely place' from the Gospels that we have considered – maybe desert, mountain or garden – and replay one of the episodes above. Ignatius of Loyola (1491–1556) invites you to engage with such texts using your five senses and your imaginations vividly. Ignatius says you should use your eyes to look at the scene, visualize it, imagine it in your mind's eye, place yourself into the picture and become one of the characters. Reach out in your imagination and touch with your fingertips the characters, the soil, the water, the physical aspects. Even smell the scents of the scene and taste the air, the food, the atmosphere. But above all, Ignatius says, open your ears and listen to what the characters are saying to each other, what they are saying to you and what God is saying to you through all this. This approach to Scripture once again slows us down and demands time and attention. It leads to clearer discernment of God's will for us in the practice of ministry. Close with St Ignatius's own prayer:

> Take, O Lord, and receive my entire liberty, my memory, my understanding and my whole will. All that I am and all that I possess You have given me: I surrender it all to You to be disposed of according to Your will. Give me only Your love and Your grace; with these I will be rich enough.[8]

Further reading

O. Cullmann, *Prayer in the New Testament* (London: SCM Press, 1995).

J. Jeremias, *The Prayers of Jesus* (SCM Press, London, 1974).

B. C. Lane, *The Solace of Fierce Landscapes: Exploring Desert and Mountain Spirituality* (Oxford: Oxford University Press, 1998).

A. Louth, *Theology and Spirituality*, 5th edn (Oxford: SLG Press, 2000).

A. Louth, *The Wilderness of God* (London: Darton, Longman & Todd, 2003).

M. A. McIntosh, *Mystical Theology: The Integrity of Spirituality and Theology* (Oxford: Blackwell, 1998).

E. H. Peterson, *The Contemplative Pastor: Returning to the Art of Spiritual Direction* (Grand Rapids, MI: Eerdmans, 1993).

3

Jesus the rebel

The prophetic and subversive in ministry

The Galilee of Jesus' time suffered the double trouble of oppression and poverty. Sang Hyun Lee writes: 'Galileans . . . were oppressed, dehumanized and looked down upon. Galileans were marginalized by foreign invaders and also by the Jerusalem Temple-state.'[1] But above all it was a place of deep poverty and need. The Galileans were crippled by heavy taxes: dues were owed to the Roman occupier, and Temple taxes added to the burden. At the time of Jesus ordinary families were being forced to quit their ancestral landholdings, where they had lived for centuries, to meet these demands. Land was also confiscated for the building projects and villas of the urban elite at Sepphoris and Tiberias. But then they had to pay rent for what had been their own fields and homes – they became caught in a downward economic spiral, becoming tenants in their own property. We should note how many of Jesus' parables speak of absentee landlords who impose severe dues on their tenants (see, for example, Luke 16.1–8; Matt. 25.14–30). Tax and rent robbed the Galilean peasant farmer of two-thirds of the family income. Many were living at barely subsistence level. No doubt Matthew preserves an original aspect of the Lord's Prayer when he puts it: 'Forgive us our debts, as we also have forgiven our debtors' (Matt. 6.12).

As we encountered in Sepphoris, Greco-Roman culture nourished the creation of an upper class, the social elites who owned great homes and estates. The value and belief system of the culture manifested itself in indulgent architecture, which archaeology has recently revealed. Wealth was power, and the gentry of Tiberias and Sepphoris were at the top of the social pyramid. It was a world of 'haves' and 'have nots'.

It is against this background that we see, at the time of Jesus, the emergence of two significant expressions of resistance and protest against the status quo. First there were the terrorists. 'Have you come out with swords and clubs to arrest me as though I were a bandit?' (Mark 14.48). The Greek word *lestes*, translated 'bandit', denotes freedom fighter or even terrorist. Josephus tells us about revolutionary activists based in Galilee who sought to undermine Roman domination by acts of sabotage or terrorism. Since the revolt of Judas the Galilean in 4 BC, the region had become a hotbed of resistance to increasingly stifling imperial rule.[2] In the accounts of the passion it is clear that Jesus is on trial before the Roman authorities precisely for being a subversive social revolutionary. He is arraigned beside the insurrectionist Barabbas. He is crucified between two 'thieves' or 'robbers' – the tame translation of some versions (see, for example, Mark 15.27 in AV, ESV, NASB, REB), but the Greek word 'bandit' reminds us of this growing movement of rebellion and insurgency against Roman oppression.

The second group we encounter at this time were the Zealots. The hand-picked band of disciples included Judas Iscariot – his surname may relate to the Sicarri rebels, forerunners of the Zealots. Also we meet 'Simon the Zealot' and the 'sons of thunder'. Maybe, therefore, a third of the Twelve were involved one way or another in the protest movement that was raising steam at the time of Jesus. Peter Walker writes: 'The Palestine in which Jesus grew up was . . . politically red-hot . . . The tension between the Jews and Roman rulers was increasing . . . Jesus [found himself] in a context that was like a tinderbox waiting to go up in flames.'[3]

Scholars speak increasingly of Jesus as a fearless rebel. For John Dominic Crossan, Jesus is a social revolutionary who questions Rome's claims, while for Marcus Borg he is a revolutionary mystic.[4] Richard Horsley sees the Jesus movement as a peasant revolt, calling the community back to Mosaic covenantal co-operation and mutuality.[5] Sean Freyne too notes that aspects of Jesus' ministry read like a Galilean protest movement.[6] Jesus' heart was with the underdog and the oppressed Galilean peasant. He may be called an outlaw, defined as a person who rebels against established rules or practices; a nonconformist. Was he a rogue, a mischievous rascal, ready to undermine the establishment with a subversive message?

Scholars point out that the one subject most likely to lead to conflict with the Roman authorities is the question of rule – and Jesus frames his message precisely around the concept of the reign of God. What would life look like if God, not Caesar, were on the throne?[7] He challenges both the power of Rome and the conventions of first-century Judaism by his message about the kingdom of God, where all are welcome and all are equal. The kingdom of God represents a new way of living, a different path, an alternative vision for society, and the Sermon on the Mount reads like a radical manifesto. It all seems like defiance. Jesus *is* a rebel in the eyes of Rome and crucifixion is the imperial reward for insurgents: the murderous insurrectionist Barabbas was released, while Jesus hung. In contrast to the brutal strategy of the guerrilla fighters and activists, crucified to left and right, Jesus becomes a rebel by peacefully advancing the reign of God. He, the non-violent one, is pinned to the cross, between the violent alternatives.

In what ways, then, does Jesus emerge as a rebel? While the Gospels tell us that he met his death as a rebel against Rome, they communicate his subversive ministry through a closely linked image: Jesus the prophet. So what is a prophet and how is it related to rebel?

Those on the Emmaus road spoke of 'Jesus of Nazareth, who was a prophet mighty in deed and word before God and all the people' (Luke 24.19). The prophets of old both spoke the word of God and also embodied or symbolized the word in dramatic action. Jesus speaks and he acts. The burden of the Old Testament prophets was not prediction of the future, rather declaring God's word into the present situation, naming the idols and illusions of contemporary society. For example, Amos was concerned to deliver his people from self-satisfying rituals and self-absorbing forms of prayer and alert them to the desperate needs of the society around them:

I hate, I despise your festivals . . .
But let justice roll down like waters,
And righteousness like an ever-flowing stream

(Amos 5.21, 24)

In similar vein Isaiah is uncompromising:

Is this not the fast that I choose:
   to loosen the bonds of injustice,
   to undo the thongs of the yoke,
   to let the oppressed go free . . .
Is it not to share your bread with the hungry . . . ?

(Isa. 58.6–7)

Walter Brueggemann, in his classic *The Prophetic Imagination*, tells us that the role of the prophet is to envision an alternative consciousness and open up for people a different vision of things. Jesus' kingdom of God directly questioned the prevailing status quo of the kingdom of Rome. The role of the prophet is to enable an alternative perspective, which may be subversive, questioning, compassionate, and certainly reveals itself in countercultural life-style and political choices.[8]

There are three contexts in which Jesus is depicted as a radical prophet: personal, pastoral and political.

Prophet Jesus: personal self-reference

In the synagogue at Nazareth, at the very start of his public ministry, Jesus chooses a text from the prophet Isaiah to be the manifesto for his ministry: he too is called 'to bring good news to the poor . . . to proclaim release to the captives' (Luke 4.17–21).

Also in Nazareth, according to all four Gospels, Jesus calls himself a prophet in the words: 'Prophets are not without honour, except in their home town, and among their own kin, and in their own house' (Mark 6.4; Luke 4.24; John 4.44). In a further self-reference he talks about the destiny of prophets to die in the holy city: 'Yet today, tomorrow, and the next day I must be on my way, because it is impossible for a prophet to be killed away from Jerusalem' (Luke 13.33).

At the event sometimes called the 'cleansing of the temple', Jesus quotes Jeremiah and Isaiah and thereby locates himself in the tradition of Jerusalem prophets (Isa. 56.7; Jer. 7.11). This event, we know, is best interpreted as a prophetic action declaring in word and deed the ending of the temple worship. Jesus was identified by his own disciples as a prophet at Caesarea Philippi: 'And they said, "Some say [he is] John the Baptist, but others Elijah, and still others Jeremiah or one of the prophets"' (Matt. 16.14).

Prophet Jesus: pastoral context

A second context in which Jesus is greeted as a prophet is the pastoral encounter. At Nain, after he has spoken words of hope to a grieving widow and lifted up her dead son to new life, the people 'glorified God, saying, "A great prophet has risen among us!"' (Luke 7.16). Jacob's Well witnesses the woman's acclamation: 'Sir, I see that you are a prophet' (John 4.19). In Jerusalem he is hailed in prophetic terms: 'So they said again to the blind man, "What do you say about him? It was your eyes he opened." He said, "He is a prophet"' (John 9.17).

Prophet Jesus: political context

A third context can loosely be called political. At the Palm Sunday entry into Jerusalem the crowds were saying, 'This is the prophet Jesus from Nazareth in Galilee' (Matt. 21.11). Soon afterwards, we read, 'They wanted to arrest him, but they feared the crowds, because they regarded him as a prophet' (Matt. 21.46).

In the fourth Gospel Jesus is twice acclaimed a prophet in a context about political choices. 'When the people saw the sign that he had done, they began to say, "This is indeed the prophet who is to come into the world"' (John 6.14). There was a division among the people: 'When they heard these words, some in the crowd said, "This is really the prophet"' (John 7.40).

Four things stand out in Jesus' courageous and audacious prophetic ministry: he emerges as rebel, ringleader, revolutionary and radical.

Rebel Jesus: standing against culture

There is a place, Jesus shows, for righteous anger. He is outraged at cultural injustices. In first-century society children were regarded as nobodies. When Jesus saw the disciples themselves shooing away and banishing children, the account says: 'he was indignant' (Mark 10.14). The Greek verb is 'to feel irritation, to be vexed, displeased or angry at a thing'.[9] Incensed, Jesus turns these rejected ones into those who will teach us about the kingdom: 'whoever does not receive the kingdom of God as a little child will never enter it' (Mark 10.15). In an act of deepest affirmation he lays his hands on these so-called 'worthless' children and blesses them.

Jesus also gets angry at the exclusion of a leper walking alone along a road. Ancient manuscripts translating Mark 1.40 say that at the sight of the leper Jesus was 'moved with anger'. He found it intolerable, totally unacceptable, that this man should be ostracized and stigmatized by society. His next response is 'Jesus stretched out his hand and touched him' (1.41). He embraces the ones society deems untouchable and contaminating. We glimpse a Jesus who is vehemently opposed to oppression and 'structural sin' – prejudices embedded in the culture – and expresses his feelings of anger and exasperation openly.

As we have seen, Jesus embraces the poor, defying customs, smashing taboos, breaking conventions, destroying barriers and crossing all sorts of boundaries that keep people apart in strict social hierarchies. He is truly a rebel spirit!

Ringleader Jesus: empowering disciples

It is a remarkable feature of Mark's Gospel that very early on in the narrative, Jesus empowers his disciples to go out and advance his mission. Indeed, Mark tells us the reason he appointed the twelve apostles was 'to be with him, and to be sent out to proclaim the message, and to have authority to cast out demons' (Mark 3.14–15). Jesus here is not a substitute but an energizer – the exemplar, not a stand-in. It is not a question of just admiring what Jesus does but rather a question of getting on and doing it too. So he sends them out, two by two (Mark 6.7–13). Mark tells us that they are to travel light, taking nothing for the journey except a staff – they are to travel trusting in God's providence. They are to focus their ministry on the needs of the outcasts: the demonized and the sick (Mark 6.13).

Luke (10.1) tells us that Jesus commissions and despatches some 70 people – an echo of the prophet Moses and his 70 co-workers (Num. 11.16). Jesus emerges as a ringleader – one who leads others and imparts to them a real sense of authority and urgency that takes them on to the road. Luke tells us that they are to have just one message: 'The kingdom of God has come near to you' (10.9). They are to proclaim a different reign, an alternative to Roman ideology and domination: they are to declare the sovereignty of God.

Revolutionary Jesus: undermining military mindset

The two Palm Sunday processions vividly express the contrast.[10] From the east comes Jesus, sitting on a donkey, hailed as a king by children waving palms. From the west comes Pilate, arriving with a battalion of hundreds of soldiers to oversee the Passover crowds, with the sound of metal against leather, marching boots, war horses and stallions; swords and shields, standards lifted high. Pilate, coming from his headquarters in Caesarea Maritima, represents the might of Rome, ready to crush in an instant any trace of trouble or protest; Jesus comes not in a 'triumphal entry' – as it is sometimes called – but in a prophetic action, bespeaking another kingdom, a different way of doing things, an alternative vision. Jesus' action is indeed a protest against Roman might: what is it like to be people of a different king?

Scholars remind us that the Caesars, who were becoming divinized, were underpinning their claims with a sort of imperial theology: Augustus Caesar was hailed as 'son of God', his victories were announced as 'Gospel' or 'Good News'. We recall that it was precisely at Caesarea Philippi, where Herod had built a splendid new temple to the divine Augustus, that Jesus dares to ask: 'Who do you say that I am?'

Scholars see Jesus as a social rather than a political revolutionary. He refuses that option: 'When Jesus realized that they were about to come and take him by force to make him king, he withdrew again to the mountain by himself' (John 6.15). He did not want to be a conquering hero vanquishing Rome by might. He did not come to lead a political revolution but rather to call members of society back to being a covenantal egalitarian community, marked by mutual respect.

This was essentially a seditious message because it undermined the status quo and the very assumptions of Roman rule. The admonition to love your enemy and turn the other cheek directly confronts the Roman military mindset where might is right (Matt. 5.44). The word 'subversive', from the Latin *subvertere*, literally means 'to turn from under, from below, from beneath', and the parables emerge as subversive wisdom. The parable of the labourers in the vineyard (Matt. 20.1–16) affirms the worth of each person, while the advice to make peace with an opponent on the way to court (Matt. 5.25) rejects a judgemental spirit between people. As in the case of the parable of the vineyard (Mark 12), sometimes the hearers get the point and realize that 'he had told [the] parable against them' (v. 12).

Radical Jesus: critiquing Judaism

In John 3, Jesus does not say to Nicodemus, respected member of the Sanhedrin and 'a leader of the Jews' (v. 1), that he should revise or update his thinking; rather he says to this representative figure that those seeking the kingdom of God must be born again (v. 3). Jesus calls the practitioners of Judaism back to the basics: Nicodemus is next seen at the womb–tomb (John 19.39–42). Jesus emerges as a rebel or radical in relation to prevailing aspects of Judaism, represented in scribe, Pharisee and Sadducee. Though the diatribes and woes of Matthew 23 reflect the struggles that the Matthean church was facing, aspects of the radical critique of Jewish practice here no doubt go back to Jesus himself. In Matthew, Jesus calls his co-religionists 'you brood of vipers' (3.7; 12.34; 23.33), while in John, they are 'from your father the devil' (8.44). John's Gospel too reflects both the Johannine conflict with Judeans and something of Jesus' own struggle.

What is beyond doubt is that Jesus exposes hypocrisy and double standards. This is not the conflict between law and grace but an incisive critique of practices that have become distorted: 'You tithe mint, dill, and cummin, and have neglected the weightier matters of the law: justice and mercy and faith' (Matt. 23.23). As Matthew presents it, Jesus is outraged and stunned by empty rituals and the longing in his heart is to call his hearers back to real encounter with the living God. The Sermon on the Mount contrasts human traditions and divine imperatives. Radicalizing, it strikes right at the heart of the matter. 'You have heard that it was said, "You shall not commit adultery." But I say to you that everyone who looks at a woman with lust has already committed adultery with her in his heart' (Matt. 5.27–28). Jesus' prophetic critique goes to the very root and to the origin of our weakness: the relation of the human heart with God and others.

Priest as rebel: six contemporary challenges

Subversive worship

How courageously does our worship question the culture in which we find ourselves? Two opposite approaches – inculturation or being countercultural – were summed up for me at a recent meeting. An evangelical colleague explained how the clergy had abandoned clerical attire for their services, wear T-shirts and jeans, use the latest IT gadgetry, sing contemporary songs – it sounded like 'cafe church' (without the coffee). I said my church was probably totally opposite. We were culturally irrelevant, in a sense. We want to offer people things they can't get in a supermarket or in the cathedrals of our age, the shopping malls. We seek worship that is transcendent, gives a glimpse of heaven, is otherworldly and takes your breath away with its sheer beauty and mystery with its incense, icons, music, silences, darkness, symbols and sacraments! Each church was responding to the culture – the first, ministering to students, the second to older and well-travelled people. The challenge is, of course, to communicate in our worship a different vision, an alternative view of the universe, a distinctive, God-centred approach to life in contemporary society.

As we shall see in Chapter 5, the Eucharist can become subversive and opens up an alternative vision that questions and doubts the norms of society. The Eucharist emerges as profoundly counter-cultural: accepting all people as they are, scorning societal norms and hierarchies in the welcome extended to all, without distinction – a challenge to today's *X Factor* climate, where only the beautiful and clever count! The gospel itself is subversive as it throws up radical questions about our culture.

Alternative lifestyle

Perhaps one of the greatest challenges facing us is that we have accommodated unthinkingly to the spirit of the age, and our outward lives don't look very different from those around us. We are infected by the plague of individualism and the mindset of the consumer. We should grapple with ethical issues in the pulpit, shining gospel light into contemporary dilemmas. Priests should model in their household a lifestyle that questions the status quo of society. The hardest thing is to live simply.[11]

We need to learn the art of rebellion in relation to aspects of the culture that the gospel must critique. We need to train people to laugh at and scorn the advertising inflicted on us, that tries to convince us of the need for a luxury item where there is none. More seriously, we need to support people to stand up and be counted on issues that undermine the sanctity of life and inalienable human rights. But there are contentious or confusing issues where the Spirit may be speaking to us through God's world and not through synods. This happens sometimes! We have to read 'what the Spirit is saying to the churches' (Rev. 2.7) on issues like human sexuality: sometimes God might be calling out to us through the experience of those who have been alienated and despised.

In the face of materialistic, consumerist ways of living, the Church is challenged afresh to pioneer lifestyles that are different, alternative, in tune with the gospel, which indeed will go against the grain, against the flow and be countercultural in this present age.[12] Postmodernism exposes the moral and spiritual vacuum at the heart of Western society. We must be alert to the emptiness of current hedonism and to a sense of spiritual bankruptcy that cries out for experience of God revealed in a lifestyle marked by authenticity and simplicity. Dare to be different!

John Dear puts it:

> Following Jesus today in a land of nuclear weapons, rampant racism, and widespread economic injustice means actively going against our culture of violence. As the culture promotes violence, we promote Jesus' nonviolence. As the culture calls for war, we call for Jesus' peace. As the culture supports racism, sexism, and classism, we demand Jesus' vision of equality, community and reconciliation. As the culture insists on vengeance and execution, we pray with Jesus for forgiveness and compassion. As the culture summons us to be successful, to make money, to have a career, to get to the top, and to be number one, we race in the opposite direction and go with Jesus into voluntary poverty, powerlessness, humility, suffering and death. Discipleship to Jesus, according to the Gospel, requires that we love our enemies, demand justice for the poor, seek liberation of the oppressed, visit the sick and the imprisoned ... create community, beat swords into ploughshares ... If we try to engage in these social practices, we will feel the sting of discipleship and the Gospel will come alive.[13]

Prophetic struggle

The Anglican Ordinal states that priests 'are to proclaim the word of the Lord and to watch for the signs of God's new creation. They are to be messengers, watchmen and stewards of the Lord.' This image of watchmen or sentinels calls priests to be on a state of high alert, keeping constant vigil, watching for and interpreting the signs of the times: 'Upon your walls, O Jerusalem, I have set watchmen; all the day and all the night they shall never be silent. You who put the LORD in remembrance, take no rest' (Isa. 62.6, ESV).

But they are not only to be on the ramparts. An incarnational model of ministry demands that priests are down below, in the gutter and in the dirt, where the poor and wounded are to be found. They will not be in ivory towers but find themselves on ground zero, joining the struggle and standing shoulder-to-shoulder with the crushed and the little ones. This model demands that we take another look at the balance in our lives between action and contemplation, between struggle and silence. There is 'a time to keep silence, and a time to speak' (Eccles. 3.7). As Pedro Casaldáliga and José María Vigil put it:

> We are called to live contemplation in liberative activity, decoding surroundings made up of grace and sin, light and shade, justice and injustice, peace and violence, discovering in this historical process the presence of the Wind that blows where it will . . . in the wail of a child, or in the full-throated cry of a people, we try to 'listen' to God.[14]

The Archbishop of Canterbury has spoken recently of the need for a 'revolution':

> As Pope Francis has recalled so memorably, we are to be a poor church for the poor, however and wherever poverty is seen, materially or spiritually. That is a revolution. Being a poor church for the poor means . . . prophetic challenge in a country that is still able and has the resources to reduce inequality.[15]

Such a 'revolution' needs rebels who are prepared to speak prophetic words to those who have responsibility in our society.

Outspoken witness

Courageous deacons, priests and bishops from history and the present day inspire and hearten us. Deacon St Francis reveals the dilemmas of being a rebel. He was intensely loyal to the Church, submitting his Rules for papal approval and honouring priests because they bring to God's people the sacrament of love. But he defied authority not so much by his words as by modelling a radically alternative lifestyle that called into question the hedonistic capitalism of his time: 'preach the gospel always, and use words when necessary'.

England has had its share of 'turbulent priests'. The description was given to Thomas à Becket (1118–70), who resisted Henry II's attempts at controlling aspects of the Church and paid with his life. In our own day a recent successor at Canterbury, Rowan Williams, has shown how it is possible to be part of the establishment yet offer searing critique of the powers that be.[16] These examples invite us to explore how we can be prophets and poets in our own contexts. Vicars and Christian leaders are just too nice. We should be angry and outraged at poverty, exploitation and social exclusion.

Risky care

The Anglican Ordinal spells out the very foundation of ministry.

> Deacons ... are to work with their fellow members in searching out the poor and weak, the sick and lonely and those who are oppressed and powerless, reaching into the forgotten corners of the world, that the love of God may be made visible.[17]

The deacon's call is the basis, the touchstone, the starting point of all ordained ministry. The deacon is invited to be a rebel in the sense that he or she is not called to walk the corridors of power, to be at the so-called 'centre' of things, but to find a scruffy and bleeding Christ in the broken and marginalized, and to honour him in them (Matt. 25).

A prophetic spirituality can be symbolized in hands and ears. Holy hands uplifted in prayer become hands outstretched in care, hands that may become dirty, bruised, wounded. We have, as it were, two ears: one to listen to God; one to listen to the cries of the poor, the screams of the exploited – which might turn out to be the cry of God himself.

Courageous prayer

There are big questions that the pastor should be ready to ask about his or her own spirituality and prayer. Are there danger signs that my spirituality is becoming narcissistic, self-centred, closed in on itself? Is my spirituality about self-fulfilment or about empowering sacrificial living? If the measure of spiritual maturity is increasing solidarity with the hurting, an enlarging capacity for compassion, what are the signs I am maturing? Is my heart getting bigger? How far can I allow the pain of the world to enter my prayer? Does my prayer have room for the oppressions and injustices of the world? What place is there for a costly intercession that is inseparable from self-offering (does not let me 'off the hook')? Indeed, what is my under-standing of intercession? Advising the Almighty or 'coming before God with the people on your heart' (Michael Ramsey)? What place is there in my prayer for the cross – not only in terms of seeking personal forgiveness but in realizing that God suffers among us? What does Matthew 25 look like in my experience? What is the evidence? Am I drawn to the margins in any way? As Jim Wallis puts it:

> Personal piety has become an end in itself instead of the energy for social justice . . . Prophetic spirituality will always fundamentally challenge the system at its roots and offer genuine alternatives based on values from our truest religious, cultural and political traditions.[18]

Questions for reflection

1 What would your priesthood or leadership look like if you modelled it on Jesus the rebel?
2 When was the last time you were outraged or indignant about an injustice, near or far, and actually did something about it?

3 The ministry of the rebel is characterized by courage and audacity, by plain speaking and bold actions. How do these reveal themselves in your ministry?

4 Dare you be disruptive in relation to society's status quo? Do you play it safe and stay out of trouble? Dare you be a 'turbulent priest'? Do vicars always have to be 'nice'? Is your ministry predictable or tame? Do you need to recover nerve and verve?

5 What would a prophetic spirituality look like in your context?

Prayer exercise

Use your hands expressively in this prayer time in four actions. Begin by clenching your fists tight and holding them before you. Feel the tension and let these fists represent an anger or frustration that bothers you today, a situation in the world that you feel strongly about. Hold them before God in the solidarity of prayer and intercession.

Second, slowly open your downturned palms and let go of the tension. Let it fall away from you to God. In this gesture give to God any negative feelings or stresses; feel them drip out of your fingertips, as it were. Surrender the situation to God's providence and sovereignty.

Third, turn your hands upwards in a gesture of surrender to God and of receiving from God. Breathe in what God wants to give you right now – perhaps a reassurance that all will be well. Breathe in his empowering Spirit, who will give you the courage for action.

Finally, take a look at your hands. Is there an action that God is calling you to make in relation to your initial concern? What should you do as a result of this – something bold, something risky or rebellious?

Recall 2 Timothy 1.7: 'God did not give us a spirit of cowardice, but rather a spirit of power and of love and of self-discipline.' End with the Serenity Prayer: 'God grant me the serenity to accept the things I cannot change; courage to change the things I can; and wisdom to know the difference.'

Further reading

J. D. Crossan, *God and Empire: Jesus Against Rome, Then and Now* (San Francisco: HarperSanFrancisco, 2007).

J. Dear, *Jesus the Rebel: Bearer of God's Peace and Justice* (Lanham, MD: Sheed & Ward, 2000).

C. Myers, *Binding the Strong Man: A Political Reading of Mark's Story of Jesus* (Maryknoll, NY: Orbis, 2008).

M. Tully, *Four Faces: A Journey in Search of Jesus the Divine, the Jew, the Rebel, the Sage* (Berkeley, CA: Ulysses Press, 1997).

P. Wallace, *The Passionate Jesus: What we can Learn from Jesus about Love, Fear, Grief, Joy and Living Authentically* (Woodstock, VT: SkyLight Paths, 2013).

J. H. Yoder, *The Politics of Jesus* (Grand Rapids, MI: Eerdmans, 1996).

4

Jesus the mystic

Unifying vision in ministry

————•◦•◦•————

In recent years scholars, attempting to pinpoint and locate the inspiration that drives Jesus, have characterized him as a 'mystic'. In his study of the prayer life of Jesus, James Thomson identifies prayer as a crucial source of inspiration and illumination for his ministry.[1] In a more recent study, Bruce Chilton characterizes Jesus as a mystic imparting esoteric teaching: 'He had already initiated them [the disciples] into his visionary practice, but now he distilled and systemized his mystical insights . . . into a personal tradition (*a kabbalah*).'[2] Marcus Borg sees Jesus as a 'Spirit person', interpreting the long periods of prayer mentioned by Luke (6.12) as Jesus' use of contemplation or meditation.[3] Borg sees Jesus as a Jewish revolutionary mystic and affirms that his mystical experience is the best explanation for his subversive wisdom and his passion and courage as a social prophet. He believes that Jesus' radical convictions spring from his prayer experience, which was marked by a vivid sense of epiphany and divine disclosure.

Other scholars too point to the prayer life of Jesus as being the source and spring of his mission: Geza Vermes, in his *Jesus the Jew*, sees Jesus as a Galilean charismatic holy man and miracle worker in the tradition of Elijah and Elisha. Tom Wright notes the role of receptive prayer in Jesus' experience, remembering that in the return of the Seventy after their mission, within their debriefing and reflection with Christ, perspectives arising from prayer are shared: 'Jesus in prayer had seen a vision . . . [he] had seen, in mystical sight, the heavenly reality which corresponded to the earthly victories won by the 70.'[4]

In this chapter, building on our look at Jesus as hermit we will attempt to uncover glimpses of his prayer life and explore what this speaks to the practice of ministry today. What is a mystic? Is it someone who has been captivated by what Rudolf Otto, in his classic *The Idea of the Holy*, called *mysterium tremendum et fascinas*? Jean-Claude Barreau affirms: 'mysticism is an existential attitude, a way of living at a greater depth'.[5] Cheslyn Jones states: 'the mystic is in touch with an "object" which is invisible, intangible and inaccessible, beyond sensual contact'.[6] 'The Christian of the future will be a mystic, or he will not exist at all', wrote Jesuit theologian Karl Rahner, affirming that mysticism is 'a genuine experience of God emerging from the very heart of our existence'.[7]

Evelyn Underhill declares that mysticism:

> is the direct intuition or experience of God; and a mystic is a person who has, to a greater or lesser degree, such a direct experience – one whose religion and life are centred, not merely on an accepted belief of practice, but on that which he regards as first hand personal knowledge.[8]

William Wainwright, in his work *Mysticism*, notes: 'While modern English speakers use "mystical experience" to refer to a wide variety of preternatural experiences, scholars have tended to restrict the term to "unitary states".'[9] Scholars speak of mysticism in terms of an experience of 'undifferentiated unity' where there are no distinctions between human and divine, between subject and object – these are transcended in a consciousness of union with God where all is one. As we explore Jesus' mysticism we shall note some significant differences: while Jesus has a vision for the wholeness of creation, he sees this as the coming together of different elements that had been separated – their reconciliation, not their merger.

Seeing things differently

I want to explore here how, in Jesus' experience, his mystical openness to the Father is not only a question of firsthand knowledge of God but also triggers and enables a new and different way of knowing altogether – a different way of seeing the world. The essential thing about his mystical prayer, it seems, is its ability to encompass and enfold into one, into a unity, the diverse and often competing elements of life. Jesus is a seer in more than one sense.[10] He opens his eyes to view the world, its divisions and possibilities, with insight and longing.

As we have seen, Jesus goes *up into the hills* to pray. There he will glimpse a new perspective on things. On the shoreline at Capernaum and the lakeside villages, one can see either one coast of Galilee or another. It is not possible to see both opposite coasts at the same time. One can look west and see the city of Tiberias and the nearby northern shore – mainly Jewish, conservative traditional communities. Alternatively one can look east across the waters of the lake to the other side and glimpse enemy territory, the heathen and pagan land of the Decapolis – Hellenistic and Gentile lands where lurk demoniacs and unclean pigs! One may set one's eyes on one side or another – and an either/or choice is involved.

But when you climb up into the hills you see things differently. The higher you climb, the more you see – physically and mystically. You see vistas and panoramas that are able to encompass, in one single view, both sides. You can see both the safe traditional towns that Peter and the disciples dwelt in and you can see the steep looming cliffs of the Golan Heights to the east – the other side. In his experience of prayer on these very hills, Jesus glimpses a new reality. The lake does not divide, after all – it unites! Both sides, both peoples, both cultures are within the Father's embrace. It is not a question of dualistic either/or thinking. It is both/and. Note how Jesus will often say: 'let us go over to the other side'. He wants to enfold into his kingdom all sorts and conditions of people. He longs to criss-cross the lake repeatedly – there is space in the kingdom for all. Jesus develops a vision for wholeness – for the healing of divides.

Living in a polarized world

Jesus lived in a bitterly divided and polarized world. In the first century, society was falling apart and riven by conflict and opposing forces. Jew was pitted against Gentile as the Jewish people tried to maintain a ritual purity and sense of identity in a contaminated land. Zealot warred against Roman occupier. Pharisees and Sadducees were at each other's throats. The scribes and the lawyers were at loggerheads. The Essenes opposed and defied the Temple authorities. It was a fragmenting society, riven with divisions and splits in the population.

Studies in cultural anthropology and historical sociology illumine the dynamics and mindsets prevailing in first-century society, especially the status/shame divide.[11] In the society of Jesus' time, people were kept apart by a sense of hierarchy in which honour was ascribed to patriarchal families and to the well-to-do, while at the opposite end of the spectrum shame was associated with the social nobodies – not only obvious social outcasts like tax-collectors (deemed to be collaborators with the Romans) and prostitutes, but also children and women. It was a painfully polarized society in which the sick and maimed were excluded from the Temple and where those who did not 'fit' were mercilessly marginalized.

But this human tendency to divide and rule, to split things up so they can be controlled and manipulated, infected not only culture and social structures but the very structure of religious thinking itself. Even with the Hebrew Scriptures one detects dualistic thinking at times:

- Heaven is remote and God's ways distant (Isaiah 55.8–9).
- Enemies are to be slaughtered (Ps. 139.19–22).

The Gospels give evidence of dualistic thinking persisting among ordinary people:

- Sinners are to be stoned not welcomed (John 8.1–11).
- The outside of the cup is more important than the inside (Matt. 23.25).
- Outer compliance seems more respectable than the inner heart (Matt. 23.17–18).
- Tithing and religious observance are divorced from issues of justice and mercy (Matt. 23.23).
- The chosen people are superior to Gentiles (Mark 7.27).

Paul will go on to develop polarities in his theology – flesh vs spirit; works vs grace – while John's letters express a conflict and opposition between the Church and the world.

Sadly, Christian spirituality itself became infected with divisive, dualistic thinking as the early centuries embraced Platonic thought. This gave rise to disastrous polarities in Christian thinking as things were pitched against one another. Heaven was opposed to earth; the body to the spirit. Politics and prayer were to be kept separate. Sacred and secular were delineated with barriers, as if they were two separate realms, holy and unholy. The Church and the world are set against each other.

There seems to be a natural human tendency towards polarization, keeping things apart. It has to do with being in control, trying to make sense of things neatly, seeing things in black and white. But as we know, it can lead to fundamentalism, racism, homophobia, fear of the other. We feel safer when we oppose, judge, differentiate, label and compare. Today we live in a polarized world: republican vs democrat, conservative vs labour, protestant vs catholic, east vs west. Things are often said to be black or white. Bifurcation is the preferred option. It has been said that we live in a 'tit for tat universe'.[12] Computers, which increasingly rule our lives, are based on a binary system. Robert McAfee Brown calls this addiction to duality 'the great fallacy': noting how prevalent it is, he offers a strategy for overcoming it through an incarnational approach to the world.[13]

In spirituality, dualistic thinking has created unnecessary distances and opened up uncalled-for chasms. Where God is thought of as something 'out there' or 'up there', he is seen as remote and unapproachable. But Christian spirituality celebrates the God within, and the breakthrough to non-dualistic thinking comes precisely when the prayer of contemplation – mystic prayer – begins to shorten the distance between humans and God. John Macquarrie entitles his introduction to Christian mysticism *Two Worlds Are Ours*.[14] Prayer becomes the entry into a different way of knowing, an alternative way of perceiving reality. Prayer might begin with a sense of God beyond: 'Our Father who art in heaven.' But it dares to pray 'thy kingdom come' and moves to an awareness of the God within: 'Thy will be done, on earth as it is in heaven.' Jesus leads us from a dualistic view of things to a unitive understanding. He leads us to reconciliation.

A unifying vision

It is precisely in a context of prevailing dualistic mindsets that Jesus develops his radical unifying and inclusive vision of the kingdom of God. With all his heart he longs to bring all people together as one in their dignity as beloved and cherished children of God. In the holy city Jesus will cry out his heart's longing: 'Jerusalem, Jerusalem . . . How often have I desired to gather your children together as a hen gathers her brood under her wings, and you were not willing!' (Luke 13.34). Jesus' desire is for the unity of the world: 'Then people will come from east and west, from north and south, and will eat in the kingdom of God' (Luke 13.29).

Did Jesus gain this heartfelt desire from his reading of the prophet Isaiah? He was inspired by Isaiah: in Luke 4 he finds in Isaiah 61 a vivid description of his ministry, and there are clues in the Gospels that he saw in Isaiah's 'servant songs' a sketch of his unfolding vocation – for example, Isaiah 53. Isaiah reveals a longing for unity and for elements that are often divorced or separated to be united: 'The wolf shall live with the lamb, the leopard shall lie down with the kid . . . The cow and the bear shall graze' (Isa. 11.6, 7). Maybe Jesus was inspired by the psalms' non-dualistic call to worship: 'Wild animals and all cattle, creeping things and flying birds! . . . Young men and women alike, old and young together!' (Ps. 148.10, 12).

The Gospels are full of episodes in which Jesus crosses boundaries and breaks down barriers, as we saw in Chapter 3. For him the child, the social nobody, is the model of true greatness (Mark 9.33–37). The presence of women is welcomed by Jesus (Luke 8.3; 23.49) and Mary Magdalene is the first witness of the resurrection. Jesus reaches out to those marginalized by society, embracing the leper (Luke 17.10–19). In Jerusalem, as he throws down the tables of the money changers in the Temple, he welcomes the outcasts and the ritually unclean: 'The blind and the lame came to him in the temple, and he cured them' (Matt. 21.14).

Notice how many of Jesus' sayings are about overcoming separation, loss and division. He sees the potential for things once separated coming together:

- The woman is reunited with her lost coin.
- The shepherd once again embraces his sheep.
- The yeast is mixed with the flour.
- The vine is joined to the branches.
- The birds come to roost in the branches.
- Things old and new are to be treasured.
- The enemy is to be loved.
- The prodigal is restored to his father.
- The wounded Jewish traveller finds himself in the arms of a hated Samaritan.
- God's will is to be done on earth as it is in heaven.
- Love of God and love of neighbour are inseparable.
- The kingdom is both now and not yet, here and still to come.
- The life of the disciple is to be marked by action and contemplation: Martha and Mary need each other – being and doing are equally vital.

Jesus echoes the *Shema* (Deut. 6) with a holistic view of the human person: 'you shall love the Lord your God with all your heart, and with all your soul, and with all your mind, and with all your strength' (Mark 12.30).

As we will see in Chapter 5, the most significant sign of his inclusive kingdom, where barriers are overturned, is the meal at which Jesus eats with tax-collectors and sinners (Luke 5.29–32: see Luke 14.12–24). For Jesus, the open table – where everyone, regardless of shame or status, has an honoured place – expresses his readiness to smash barriers and social taboos.

Where did these ideas come from? For Jesus, the self-same mountains of prayer, the hills above Galilee, become the mountains of teaching. In Matthew's perspective Jesus goes up the mountain to teach (Matt. 5), and the Sermon on the Mount follows. But this hillside is precisely the same place where Jesus went up into the hills to pray. His teachings flow from his prayer. Three major imperatives emerge in the prayer of Jesus.

Discover both the light and the cloud

First, in his prayer atop Tabor (or Hermon), in the event we call the Transfiguration (the Greek church calls it the *metamorphosis*, the transformation), Jesus gains a unifying view of reality. He refers to it as an *orama* – 'a vision', 'that which is seen', 'a sign', 'something glimpsed' (Matt. 17.9). Jesus sees things that were separated coming together. This is not a case of dualistic either/or options or dichotomies; rather both/and conjunctions recur again and again. Five unities stand out.

First, heaven itself is joined to earth. Jesus leads the disciples up a 'high mountain' that points into the heavens, but they fall to earth with their faces on the ground (Matt. 17.6). The voice of heaven is heard: 'This is my beloved Son'. And the clamour of voices of earth are heard too as Peter cries out, insensibly, 'Let us make three tents' (Luke 9.33, esv).

Second, Jesus himself is both a transcendent figure, bathed with divine light, and an immanent figure, giving his disciples a hand as he touches them and lifts them up from the earth. Intimacy meets ultimacy. Human fear and awe meet joy in this double encounter of one who is 'beyond' yet humanly present.

Third, suffering and glory are closely intertwined: while Jesus reveals his radiant glory, Luke emphasizes that in the self-same moment he speaks with Moses about the exodus he is to accomplish in Jerusalem (Luke 9.31). The heavenly city of glory points to the earthly city of passion and pain.

A fourth unitive feature reveals itself in the presence of Moses and Elijah. They are often taken to represent, dualistically, the Jewish Law and the Prophets – the two main ways God reveals himself under the first covenant. They seem to need each other, for they appear together – the Law can become unhelpful without the prophetic critique that brings to the fore issues of honesty and justice; the Prophets need the grounding in the commandments or else they might become unanchored from the tradition. In the event of the Transfiguration, the Law and the Prophets stand in closest relation, linked by the person of Jesus who extends a hand to each.

Fifth, Jesus encounters God in both the light and the cloud. The light represents the *kataphatic* tradition of prayer – where affirmations and declarations about God are made confidently: Jesus is light; 'his face shone like the sun'; 'his garments became white as light'. But the cloud represents the *apophatic* tradition – where words give way to silence; concepts about God dissolve into speechless wonder; the unifying dense fog of the cloud shrouds the disciples and silences all attempts at talking. Peter's instinct is to construct tents – to domesticate the divine; contain the mystery; regain control in the situation. This can represent our attempts in prayer to 'get a handle' on God; box him in with words, concepts and images; encase divinity within human structures. But precisely at the point at which Peter suggests the building of booths, 'a cloud came and overshadowed them; and they were afraid as they entered the cloud' (Luke 9.34). The response to human tent-building is a divine smothering or drenching in mysterious wet mist where visibility is reduced to nil. The cloud now dampens the senses and exuberant conceptualizing, silences the overactive mind. The cloud eclipses the sun: there has been, as it were, a change in the weather, from bright sunlight to darkening cloud, gloom and impenetrable haze. A swirling fog blankets the disciples. It becomes a poignant symbol of that transition in prayer from active, discursive thinking to simpler loving. But Matthew calls it a 'bright cloud', as if the revealing light and the concealing cloud can co-exist in the vision of Jesus. In the event of the Transfiguration, Jesus unites the two ways of prayer – the two very different approaches to God – represented in light and cloud.

Discover a sacramental universe

Second, as Jesus prayed in the hills above Galilee he looked at the world sacramentally and contemplatively. 'Consider the flowers of the field' – take a long, slow look at them and discover how they reveal the secrets of the kingdom. Time and again Jesus glimpses

the unity of creation. Jesus sees a wholeness to creation – there is
no place for dualistic polarized thought.

Both/and thinking reveals itself again and again. Looking up at
the sun and feeling on his skin the rain falling on the lush Galilee
hills, Jesus announces: 'he makes his sun rise on the evil and
on the good, and sends rain on the just and on the unjust' (Matt.
5.45, ESV). Looking at the earth below him and seeing how wheat
and weed become intertwined, he declares: 'Let both of them grow
together' (Matt. 13.24–30).

For Jesus, the key is in the looking – how we see the world
contemplatively; what we notice; what we miss. Jesus rejoices:
'blessed are your eyes, for they see' (Matt. 13.16). In the *Gospel
of Thomas* (113), his disciples ask him, 'When will the kingdom
come?' Jesus replies: 'the Father's kingdom is spread out upon the
earth, and people don't see it.' In another saying from this source,
words are placed on the lips of Jesus that testify to a unifying
vision of the world: 'When you make the two into one, and when
you make the inner like the outer and the outer like the inner,
and the upper like the lower . . . then you will enter the kingdom'
(*Gospel of Thomas* 22).

Discover union with God

Third, Jesus' prayer in John 17 celebrates the unity of Father and
Son. He had already declared: 'The Father and I are one' (John
10.30); now he longs and aches for such a communion to be
established in the hearts of all. His prayer up in the hills anticipates
his intense prayer of the Upper Room as John offers it to us. In
the fourth Gospel Jesus affirms: 'Those who abide in me and I
in them bear much fruit' (15.5). In his great prayer of John 17
Jesus pleads: 'that they may all be one. As you, Father, are in
me and I am in you, may they also be in us' (17.21). He wants
to overcome the divide. This is a radically alternative way of
looking at things: to uncover and reveal the unity of all creation
with God.

Jesus' longing culminates in the cross. He is crucified on a
structure that sums up his healing of dichotomy: the vertical,

transcendent, Godward shaft of the cross meets the horizontal, inclusive arm. Outstretched arms embrace all. The Letter to the Ephesians celebrates how here Jew and Gentile are brought together: 'in his flesh he has made both groups into one and has broken down the dividing wall . . . that he might create in himself one new humanity in place of the two, thus making peace . . . through the cross' (Eph. 2.14–16). At Calvary itself, as Jesus stretches out his arms wide to embrace the world, it is astonishing to see who are the founder-members of his new community gathered at the foot of the cross: a despairing mother; a fisherman disciple; a political guerrilla (the so-called 'thief'); a soldier centurion who stands for the might of Rome; Mary Magdalene who loves much, because she is forgiven much. The space of Calvary has a place for all. The cross is a place of reconciliation, and Jesus extends his arms to encompass the universe: '[God] has made known to us the mystery of his will . . . as a plan for the fullness of time, to gather up all things in him, things in heaven and things on earth' (Eph. 1.9–10). The Letter to the Colossians affirms: 'in him all things hold together . . . through him God was pleased to reconcile to himself all things, whether on earth or in heaven, by making peace through the blood of his cross' (Col. 1.17, 20).

The vocation of the priest and leader

The vocation of the priest or Christian leader is to open up a spaciousness where all can be welcomed and treasured without distinction or fawning undue attention on the clever. I have been privileged to face this challenge in three contexts. As a parish priest I have found myself in communities where mansions and council flats are both located – overflowing wealth not far from grinding poverty. It is the vocation of a parish church to be a safe space for all – not a monolithic monochrome congregation but accurately reflecting the social diversity of the benefice, as we read in James 2.1–5: rich and poor are to be welcomed on equal terms into the Christian assembly.

Within parishes, a monthly challenge is often to create meaning-ful all-age worship that neither patronizes the young nor insults the adult. The basis of such worship is, of course, our shared baptismal identity and dignity:

> As many of you as were baptized into Christ have clothed yourselves with Christ. There is no longer Jew or Greek, there is no longer slave or free, there is no longer male and female; for all of you are one in Christ Jesus.   (Gal. 3.27–28)

As director of continuing ministerial education charged with designing training programmes for the newly ordained, the challenge was bringing black-suited Anglo-Catholics into relationship with T-shirt-wearing evangelicals. They had studied for the ordained ministry quite separately in their respective seminaries or Bible colleges. They had had few occasions to encounter each other. But where individuals find themselves equal within a learning community, breakthroughs are possible. They were not there as delegates of a tradition – they were there as fellow learners. And we found that the secret was discovering the lost art of listening to one another. We might even glimpse something new, or something of ancient wisdom!

In Jerusalem as course director of an ecumenical college the challenge was to build a learning community from a diversity of cultures representing diverse theological world views. Nigerian literalists found themselves alongside American liberals. But both were on a journey. Both were finding out what it means to be a pilgrim – which requires that self-protective walls crumble and prejudices be melted in the Middle Eastern sun. When diverse or even opposing groups found that they were being called to become not only a learning community but also a pilgrim band on the move through the Holy Land, hearts and minds were opened as they discovered on the journey contemplative and reflective spaces.

Jesus the mystic shows us that it is in the place of receptive prayer that we discover a vision for unity. We start to crave for wholeness and healing among the divided. Vision that inspires is born in mystic prayer – the sort of prayer that looks contemplatively at the world, and the sort that learns to receive from God, the Father of us all:[15]

> There is one body and one Spirit, just as you were called to
> the one hope of your calling, one Lord, one faith, one baptism,
> one God and Father of all, who is above all and through all
> and in all. (Eph. 4.4–6)

It is the task of the priest or Christian leader to dream dreams
and see visions. But in order for this to happen there must be a
receptive stillness and a readiness to push out the boundaries of
our thinking about God's kingdom so that we may perceive things
differently and with bigger vision. The Archbishop of Canterbury
has said recently: 'There has never been a renewal of church life
in western Christianity without a renewal of prayer . . . it is in
prayer, individually and together, that God puts into our minds
new possibilities of what the Church can be.'[16]

Paul calls Christian leaders 'stewards of the mysteries of God'.
The phrase, from 1 Corinthians 4.1–2, suggests that priests and
leaders will not only be guardians of the spiritual traditions of
the Church but also the ones who open these resources to others.
Priests' role as teachers of divine mysteries will spring from their
relationship with God, their glimpse of eternity and their encounter
with the Transcendent and the Incarnate One, nurtured by prayer
and silence. As Robert Barron puts it:

> If the priest is to be a mediator between heaven and earth,
> if he is to speak symbolically of the all-embracing and ever
> elusive mystery of Being itself, he must be in habitual contact
> with the Mystery, he must stand stubbornly in the presence
> of God. He must take with utmost seriousness the command
> of St Paul to pray continually, to orient the whole of his being
> to the love of God. In short, the priest must be a mystic, a
> contemplative, a person of prayer . . . who must be, in every
> fibre of his being, formed by prayer.[17]

One of the conclusions from recent research about today's spiritual climate was clear: 'We need more "contemporary mystics" . . .
who are dedicated to unpacking the hidden treasures of Christian
spirituality and teaching Christian leaders how to facilitate styles
of worship that engage with contemporary spiritual hunger.'[18]

Questions for reflection

1 What divisions among people do you face in your ministry? How can you bring these into prayer?
2 What dichotomies or divorces do you encounter today in Christian thinking or strategy? How can Christian prayer enfold and unite the diverse elements? How can you bring into a dialogue or conversation separated elements?
3 What do you make of the claim relating to Jesus by the Sea of Galilee: 'The higher you climb, the more you see – physically and mystically'? Does this resonate with your own experience of prayer?
4 This chapter claims that at the heart of mystic prayer is the ability to receive from God a unifying vision of the kingdom. How would you express the heart of mystical prayer?
5 What do you think we can learn most effectively from Jesus the mystic? What is your own vision for wholeness and healing?

Prayer exercise

Use the 'cross prayers' devised by Francis of Assisi. Open your arms wide – extend them as far as you can. This is first to embody a solidarity with the cross. Think of Jesus opening wide his arms on the cross to embrace all who suffer, all who are in any form of distress. Think of Christ's all-encompassing love and acceptance. Second, think of the risen Christ and the way he longs to enfold the whole of creation, the little ones and marginalized ones of the earth. Third, offer this prayer as an act of intercession. It is a prayer that hurts – in the sense that your arms will grow weary and ache. Moses prayed like this and had to have others hold up his arms (Exod. 17.11–12). As you feel the ache, let it connect you to those who are in pain, those who are hurting: the sick, the dispossessed, those whose human rights are trampled on. Finally, use this prayer action as an act of self-offering. Offer yourself afresh to God for the part he has in store for you in his mission of reconciliation in the world.

Further reading

C. Bourgeault, *The Wisdom Jesus: Transforming Heart and Mind – A New Perspective on Christ and his Message* (Boston: Shambhala, 2008).

R. McAfee Brown, *Spirituality and Liberation: Overcoming the Great Fallacy* (London: Hodder & Stoughton, 1988).

R. Rohr, *Everything Belongs: The Gift of Contemplative Prayer* (New York: Crossroad, 2003).

R. Rohr, *The Naked Now: Learning to See as the Mystics See* (New York: Crossroad, 2009).

5

Jesus the reveller

Festivity in ministry

The 2003 edition of the *Shorter Oxford English Dictionary* defines 'reveller' as '1 A participant in a revel, merrymaking, or festivity . . . 2 A person who takes delight in something'. Is this an appropriate designation for Jesus? And is it shocking to think of Jesus as a 'raver'? According to *Collins English Dictionary*, a raver is 'a person who leads a wild or uninhibited social life'. According to the *Merriam-Webster Learner's Dictionary*, a raver is 'someone who goes to many parties'. The *Macmillan Dictionary* has 'someone who likes to enjoy themselves, for example by going out with a lot of different people'.

What is the evidence? *Can* Jesus be properly called 'a reveller'?

- Jesus chose the party and celebratory meal as the central symbol of his message about the kingdom of God. Scholars talk of his 'open commensality' (open table) and 'radical egalitarianism'.[1]
- Jesus turns 180 gallons of water into wine, the first of his signs. In John's view this sets the tone and priority for his ministry.
- Jesus allowed women to anoint his feet or head at a dinner party. Perhaps one of them was a prostitute (Luke 7.36–50). She loved much because she was forgiven much.
- Jesus' parables about things lost and found are all marked by a joyous party: the lost sheep; the lost coin (Luke 15.3–10). Significantly, they are prefaced by the words: 'Now all the tax-collectors and sinners were coming near to listen to him. And the Pharisees and the scribes were grumbling and saying, "This fellow welcomes sinners and eats with them"' (Luke 15.1–2).

- Jesus is accused of being 'a glutton and a drunkard' (Matt. 11.19; Luke 7.34).

- Jesus keeps 'bad company'. The Pharisees ask the disciples: 'Why does your teacher eat with tax-collectors and sinners?' (Matt. 9.11; Mark 2.16).

- Jesus and the disciples feast while John the Baptist and his followers fast (Mark 2.18).

- As Marcus Borg puts it: 'This image of God [as gracious] is implicit in one of the most striking features of Jesus' ministry, namely the meals which he shared with "sinners" – that is, outcasts.'[2]

In the Gospels, Jesus never turns down an invitation to party! Luke's Gospel tells us about a series of social gatherings. In Luke 5 Jesus dines with new convert Matthew (or Levi). In chapter 7 he has dinner at Simon's house. In chapter 10 he enjoys hospitality at Martha's house. In chapter 11 he has a meal with the Pharisees; in chapter 14 he dines with another Pharisee. In chapter 19 he celebrates with Zacchaeus. And, of course, the account culminates with the Passover celebration meal in chapter 22, which includes singing! Luke's chapter 14, as we shall see, is devoted to the theme of inclusive parties.

Jesus and dance

Jesus refers to dance three times in the Gospels. In the great parable the welcome of the forgiving father to the returning prodigal son culminates and climaxes with dancing and music: it is the father who is prodigal, 'wastefully or recklessly extravagant', 'lavishly abundant'. The great party becomes the symbol in the parable of God's radical acceptance of the wayward, and of God's lavish love.

Jesus expresses his very mission in the metaphor of dance. 'But to what will I compare this generation? It is like children sitting in the marketplaces and calling to one another: "We played the flute for you, and you did not dance"' (Matt. 11.16–17; also Luke 7.32). Jesus is dismayed with the people's unresponsiveness – they will not join in the dance. I can imagine Jesus also phrasing this positively: 'The kingdom is at hand. Listen to the children! As they are piping, they call out: "Come and join in the dance!"'

This dance language appears in the Beatitudes themselves. Jesus says: 'Blessed are you when people hate you, and when they exclude you . . . on account of the Son of Man. Rejoice in that day and leap for joy, for surely your reward is great in heaven' (Luke 6.22–23; this can be translated 'dance' – the J. B. Phillips New Testament gives us 'jump for joy'). Jesus calls his disciples to dance for joy in the very hour that they are persecuted. The dance is to be the response to pain. This beatitude is an echo of Psalm 30: 'You have turned my mourning into dancing; you have taken off my sackcloth and clothed me with joy' (v. 11).

Of course, Jesus gains this delight in dancing from his Jewish heritage and culture, from family and community celebrations he enjoyed in Nazareth and Capernaum. Dancing was a frequent entertainment in such villages. The dance is still a feature of Jewish life today – not only at social occasions but in worship, as in dancing with the scrolls, the custom of Simchat Torah, the 'Rejoicing in the Law', the exuberant festive dancing procession around the synagogue that marks the end of the cycle of Jewish high holy days.

There is a rich tradition of dancing in the Hebrew Scriptures: 'there is a time to mourn, and a time to dance' (Eccles. 3.4). Miriam dances in joy at the event of the exodus (Exod. 15.20). David danced exuberantly before the Lord as he brought the Ark of the Covenant up to Jerusalem (2 Sam. 6), much to the scorn of his wife Michal. The narrative celebrates the joy: 'David and all the house of Israel were dancing before the LORD with all their might, with songs and lyres and harps and tambourines and castanets and cymbals' (v. 5).

The Psalms call on us repeatedly to dance. Psalm 149.2–3 cries out to the people: 'Let Israel be glad in its Maker; let the children of Zion rejoice in their King. Let them praise his name with dancing, making melody to him with tambourine and lyre.'

Jesus and parties

Four themes stand out in the joyous gatherings mentioned in the Gospels. We need to reflect on these and embody them in our practice of priesthood and ministry.

Celebration

Jesus invites us to rejoice in God's gifts. According to the fourth Gospel, he begins his ministry with a party – he shares in the exuberance of a wedding. Jesus' central message here is: 'I came that they may have life, and have it abundantly' (John 10.10). Stunningly, the wedding at Cana reveals God's generosity. Whether we read it as history or parable, its message is unmistakable.

We are awed by the sheer quantity of wine that John tells us Jesus produces: six stone water jars, each holding 20 or 30 gallons. In our terms, that is 1,168 bottles, of our normal 75cl size! Or 194 boxes of wine. What a party for a small village! (Archaeology reveals that the population of nearby Nazareth was about 200 at the time of Christ, and Cana was a lot smaller.) This joyous extravagance testifies to a theme John introduces in his prologue: 'From his fullness we have all received, grace upon grace' (1.16).

Revelation

But all is not what it seems. We are invited to look beneath the surface and glimpse an epiphany taking place. This is no mere event or happening, it is a *sign* – but a sign of what? To what does it point? John says: 'Jesus did this, the first of his signs, in Cana of Galilee, and revealed his glory' (John 2.11).

What is 'glory' in John's perspective? It is the visible radiance of the divine presence – a sign that God is powerfully at work. John introduces this key theme in his words: 'And the Word became flesh and lived among us, and we have seen his glory, the glory as of a father's only son, full of grace and truth' (1.14). This glory is manifested in a series of signs. But it is supremely and paradoxically to be revealed on the cross. John sees the crucifixion of Christ as the greatest moment of glorification. In the fourth Gospel, Christ can say of his passion: 'The hour has come for the Son of Man to be glorified' (John 12.23; see also 7.39; 13.31; 17.1–5). Jesus approaches his death not as a disaster to be endured but as a glory to be embraced, for the cross is the moment of salvation. And here at Cana Jesus says to Mary: 'My hour has not yet come' (2.4). Cana precipitates the dawning of the 'hour' of his passion, and will be followed by the event in the temple where the foes of Jesus already take their place in the unfolding drama. So John calls this a sign – it is symbolic, it is sacramental. What is its deeper message?

Transformation

John calls it 'the first of his signs' (2.11). The party at Cana is ultimately about God changing lives. *That* is why it is at the start of the Gospel narrative, and sets Jesus' tone for what is to follow. The changing of water into wine symbolizes Jesus' power to transform lives. He takes the stuff of ordinary life – water – and turns it into the new wine of the kingdom. Seven signs are mentioned in the fourth Gospel: changing water into wine (2.1–11); healing the official's son in Capernaum (4.46–54); healing the paralytic at Bethesda (5.1–18); feeding the 5,000 (6.5–14); Jesus' walk on water (6.16–24); healing the blind at birth (9.1–7); raising of Lazarus (11.1–45). All involved in these episodes testify to the transformation Christ brings, changing lives for ever and healing the deepest needs of humanity.

Inclusion

This is the dominant theme of the parties in Luke's Gospel. His open table becomes the pre-eminent symbol of the kingdom. In contrast to the hierarchies of Roman society and the polarities of Jewish society, shaped by the purity laws that declared the maimed and sick to be outcast, Jesus' parties have a radical message, welcoming all without exception. In his parable, as 'respectable' people turn down party invitations, the king says:

> Go out at once into the streets and lanes of the town, and bring in the poor, maimed, blind and lame . . . Go out to the roads and lanes, and compel people to come in, so that my house may be filled. (Luke 14.21, 23)

Earlier Jesus was insistent: 'when you give a banquet, invite the poor, the crippled, the lame, and the blind. And you will be blessed, because they cannot repay you' (Luke 14.13–14).

The most significant sign of his inclusive kingdom, where barriers are overturned, is the meal at which Jesus eats with tax-collectors and sinners (Luke 5.29–32: see 14.12–24). For Jesus, the open table – where everyone, regardless of shame or status, has an honoured place – expresses his readiness to smash barriers and social taboos. His rave-like party behaviour is certainly unconventional, for it breaks the cultural conventions and expectations of his time. Marcus Borg puts it: 'the simple act of sharing a meal had exceptional religious and social significance in the social world of Jesus. It became a vehicle of cultural protest, challenging the ethos and politics of holiness.'[3] Jesus welcomes the impure, the social outcast; he thereby declares the unacceptable and stigmatized as accepted and loved by God.

John the Seer will go on to depict universal salvation in terms of a great banquet or party in heaven: 'And the angel said to me, "Write this: Blessed are those who are invited to the marriage supper of the Lamb"' (Rev. 19.9). Our ultimate vocation is expressed as an invitation to a party!

Fiesta in the local church

Brother Roger of Taizé cried out: 'Restore to pastors a spirit of festival!'[4] If a key task of the Christian leader or priest is to create inclusive community, the local church needs to allow festivity to course through its lifeblood and should be famous, or even infamous, in the neighbourhood for the generosity of its welcome and its extraordinary embrace of the other. The priest has the privilege of being a catalyst for risky, open-hearted and costly hospitality, which communicates the heart of the gospel more powerfully and effectively than a thousand sermons. Not a jolly, superficial parish social but a healing and restorative gathering that generates acceptance of outsider and is balm to the wounded. We could learn from Christians in Latin America. Pedro Casaldáliga and José María Vigil write:

A sort of 'state of fiesta' can be interwoven, in a logic that defies rules and prejudices, with work, suffering, prayer ... Festivals are also pluriform expressions of meeting and communicating ... of myths and memories, of eating and drinking, of faith and sensuality, of utopia and satire ... a culture shock for those unable to understand the amalgam of mourning and laughing, drinking and believing, death and vitality, that these celebrations involve.[5]

The Eucharist reveals the Church as it should be: a community of faith in which different gifts and ministries are exercised. The Eucharist can be a place of profound affirmation for the priest as priestly identity and a celebratory, festive role are summed up vividly in the various actions – what the priest or deacon does in church is to be done also outside in the community and in the world. The revelling Eucharist reveals the very mission of the priest. There are ten particular moments that are most symbolic and iconic of the priestly ministry and our mission, which should be celebratory and joyous, even exuberant, and festive in character.[6]

Proclamation of the gospel: the deacon or priest is not here giving another reading but is proclaiming the word of life, and all stand to listen to the voice of the living Christ. This encapsulates the very mission of the ordained: to speak out boldly the message of salvation; to proclaim good news.

Confession and absolution: the priest declares the forgiveness and radical acceptance of God – a moment of profound joy and affirmation for all. And the priest is to reveal such a non-judgemental embrace in daily ministry.

Intercession: in the prayers, God's people offer themselves for involvement in God's mission. It is the moment in the celebration at which priest and people are reminded of their vocation to be in touch with the passionate and compassionate heartbeat of God and with the pulse of a world in need of healing. Every Eucharist should include the voices of the young and, in one way or another, the cries of the poor.

Sign of peace: as the priest calls God's people to share a sign of mutual acceptance and reconciliation, around the table Christ forms a people in radical equality, community and dignity. Here we are offered a powerful image of our vocation to be reconcilers and agents of God's healing in a broken, fragmenting world. The Sign of Peace declares that all are valued, all have dignity, all belong.

Offertory: as priests receive the people's bread – 'which earth has given and human hands have made' – at the holy table, so they seek to lead people to surrender their daily work and labour to God. As priests accept the wine, so throughout the week in parish ministry they will be helping people bring their sorrows and joys to God: the chalice holds 'wine to gladden the human heart' (Ps. 104.15) but also represents the cup of suffering (Mark 14.36). Taking in their hands these elements of creation, they will be seeking to live out daily in the world a Christian approach to creation, a sacramental view of the universe, seeing all creation as God-bearing and God-revealing.

Thanksgiving: the priest, inviting God's people to 'lift up their hearts', seeks to live a Eucharistic life, marked by daily praise, fulfilling the injunction to 'pray without ceasing, give thanks in all circumstances' (1 Thess. 5.17–18).

Consecration: as the priest prays that by the power of the Holy Spirit the natural elements of bread and wine may become for us the body and blood of Christ, so we see a powerful image of God's call to us to surrender into his hands the raw material of our lives, that we may become Christ-bearers for our needy world. We find ourselves caught up into the movement of Christ's self-offering to the Father as we make *anamnesis* (remembrance) of the Cross.

Fraction: in the breaking of the bread, priests see before their very eyes the clearest possible expression of the ministry: to be consecrated for God and to be broken and given for the people. As the ordination rite in the Catholic tradition puts it, at the giving of the Chalice: 'Realize what you are doing; imitate what you handle.'

Communion: as priests discover the presence of Christ, in some way, in fragments of broken bread and in poured out wine, so they seek to fulfil the injunction in Matthew 25, 'I was sick and you visited me', finding Christ in broken, fragile bread-like lives. The Eucharist, celebrating 'God with us' and 'the Word made flesh' in the physicality and materiality of created elements, prompts us to go out into God's world and become ever more alert to God's presence in human lives – to rediscover the sacramentality of all of life. St John Chrysostom asks:

> Do you wish to honour the body of Christ? Do not ignore him when he is naked. Do not pay him homage in the temple clad in silk, only then to neglect him outside where he is cold and ill-clad. He who said: 'This is my body' is the same who said: 'You saw me hungry and you gave me no food', and 'whatever you did to the least of my brothers you did also to me . . .' What good is it if the Eucharistic table is overloaded with golden chalices when your brother is dying of hunger? Start by satisfying his hunger and then with what is left you may adorn the altar as well.
>
> (Homily on the Gospel of Matthew 50.3–4)

Further, as priests offer Holy Communion to God's people, they will see in this action a reminder of the call to go out into the world to respond to both the physical and spiritual hungers: to feed the poor and the spiritually hungry of the parish.

Blessing: as priests bless the people and send them forth into mission, so they are reminded of their vocation to bless and empower people's lives daily, helping to enable and resource the ministry of all God's people.

In these ways elements within the Eucharist can energize mission and remind us all of the celebratory and festive character of the banquet at the table of the kingdom, the altar of the Lord. At the very heart of the Eucharist is the joyous celebration of the cross, passion and resurrection of the Lord. It is the paschal mystery, the mystery of Easter, the mystery of God's sharing and redeeming our human pain that will help make sense of the daily practice of ministry – it is the key, the heart of parish ministry. What is proclaimed in the Eucharist – in both word and sacrament – is nothing less than the very message we will live out in our daily mission. The Eucharist clarifies and strengthens the vocation of the priest. If one may, in some way, act *in persona Christi* at the Lord's table, this is only to remind us that we are to do the same on the street, in the parish, in the home.

We need to be more alert and aware at each celebration of the working of the Holy Spirit. Christopher Irvine puts it: 'to elucidate the formational meaning of worship we need to work with a more developed pneumatology . . . and accordingly give a greater logical priority to the presence and active working of God'.[7] The Eucharist is not just 'another service to be taken' but a life to be lived – for in it, as in all worship, God invites us to formation and transformation by the Holy Spirit. The Eucharist powerfully reminds us, on each occasion, of our mission and vocation. St Augustine puts it:

> If you, therefore, are Christ's body and members, it is your own mystery that is placed on the Lord's table! It is your own mystery that you are receiving! You are saying *Amen* to what you are: your response is a personal signature, affirming your faith. When you hear *The Body of Christ* you reply *Amen*. Be a member of Christ's body, that your *Amen* may ring true!
>
> (Sermon 272)

We must ensure that every Eucharist is characterized by a blend of celebration and solidarity – every celebration should be life-affirming and life-empowering. The Eucharist should reflect the joyous meals of Jesus and his message of liberation and acceptance. Above all, it should be remembered that every Sunday is a day of resurrection. Let fiesta break out! John of Damascus (675–749) exults:

> Now let the heavens be joyful,
> And earth her song begin,
> The round world keep high triumph,
> And all that is therein;
> Let all things seen and unseen
> Their notes of gladness blend,
> For Christ the Lord is risen,
> Our joy that hath no end.

Brother Roger puts it:

> Festival is a small field that each of us has to cultivate
> within oneself, a tiny playground for exercising freedom and
> spontaneity ... In every person lies a zone of solitude that
> no human intimacy can fill: and there God encounters us.
> There, in that depth, is set the intimate festival of the risen
> Christ. So henceforth, in the hollow of our being, we dis-
> cover the risen Christ: he is our festival ... the risen Christ
> makes of a person's life a continual festival.[8]

Questions for reflection

1 Celebration: how can we make our worship more celebratory
and outward-looking and less introspective and sin-preoccupied?
2 Revelation: in what ways does your ministry give out 'signs' of
God's love and welcome?
3 Transformation: celebrate how people are being changed
through your ministry – notice little differences, and give
thanks.
4 Inclusion: how truly inclusive is your church? Is there any local
group or population not represented in your congregation?

Prayer exercise

With others, design a Eucharistic celebration that incorporates
clearly the four elements of revelling or festivity identified here.
Be prepared to push the boundaries a little so you can bring fresh
emphasis to certain elements within the liturgy.

Further reading

R. Greenwood, *Practising Community: The Task of the Local Church*
(London: SPCK, 1996).
D. Lonsdale, *Listening to the Music of the Spirit: The Art of Discernment*
(Notre Dame, IN: Ave Maria Press, 1992).

P. McPartlan, *The Eucharist Makes the Church* (Edinburgh: T. & T. Clark, 1993).

J. Walling, *Daring to Dance with God: Stepping into God's Embrace* (Brentwood, TN: Howard Books, 2000).

A. Wingate, *Free to Be: Discovering the God of Freedom* (London: Darton, Longman & Todd, 2000).

6

Jesus the jester

Unnerving hilarity in ministry

'Jesus began to weep' (John 11.35). We often think of Jesus as the 'man of sorrows' (Isa. 53.3, alternative reading). We recall him shedding tears over Jerusalem (Luke 19.41). We often think of him as serious and solemn. But if we turn to the Gospel of Thomas, which many scholars date to the first century and accept as an early collection of Jesus' sayings, again and again we see the line: 'Jesus laughed'.

When the Gospel is read out in church services, the deacon or reader normally puts on his or her most gloomy face as they read the appointed passage. Indeed, some traditions direct that the Gospel be read 'solemnly' – that was the rubric or instruction. And often the congregation put on their longest faces and greet the reading in mournful tones, saying 'Praise to Christ the Lord'. But when Jesus first uttered the words they would often be greeted by howls of laughter and roars of glee! He often used funny turns of phrase to get his hearers thinking – they would first laugh; then the penny dropped and they would get the often serious point. Ripples of laughter would spread through the crowd. Jesus emerges as a jester, a joker, a man with a twinkle in his eye, a fun-loving guy who doesn't mind telling jokes to make a good point.

The image of Christ the clown recently rediscovered

First, in his study *The Feast of Fools* the Harvard scholar Harvey Cox called us to take a serious look at this icon of Christ. He suggests that there are periods in the life of the Church when the image of Christ as jester, troubadour, harlequin or clown becomes

urgent and necessary. When the Church tries to be in power, upholding the establishment and the status quo, Christologies such as
Christ the King or Judge are used to justify its position. But when
it is persecuted or marginalized and finds itself in a countercultural place, it is better able to subvert conventional wisdom and
question existing norms. This is the very function of a clown.[1]

Second, recent research by the Jesus Seminar group of scholars
led by Robert Funk has highlighted the ways the sayings and
parables of Jesus open up a fresh way of seeing reality: 'Jesus may
be described as a comic savant. He was perhaps the first stand-
up Jewish comic. A comic savant is a sage who embeds wisdom
in humour.'[2] In his study *Honest to Jesus*, Funk analyses how
the rhetorical approach of Jesus as teacher employs humour and
playfulness that both relax and attack! In one of his favourite
approaches – hyperbole – Jesus plays with words that trigger
laughter with their outrageous exaggeration.

Crazy words

What forms of humour does Jesus employ? What is Jesus aiming
to do? I notice four functions of humour in the Gospels that may
be appropriate in the expression of ministry today.

Jesus in his clowning calls us to re-imagine and reframe

We use the word 'reframe' – putting the situation into a different
frame or interpretative context. The parables trigger and stimulate
a paradigm shift: they shift perceptions and help people look at
things differently. For example, the parable of the Good Samaritan
up-ends our usual logical thinking and subverts our normal
responses: here it is the despised who ministers, and the despising
learns to receive!

In Mark's perspective, Jesus at the outset announces his intention to revolutionize and radically shake up people's thinking. 'The
time is fulfilled, and the kingdom of God has come near; repent,
and believe in the good news' (Luke 19.42). So the opening lines
of Jesus' proclamation entail a call to 'repent'. We usually read this
in a moralistic way, calling us to penitence, but as recent writers

have reminded us, this is in fact a summons to an utterly different way of seeing reality.[3] The word is literally *meta*, meaning 'beyond' or 'large', and *noia*, which translates as 'mind'. Jesus is calling us to 'go beyond the mind' or 'go into the big mind'. He is inviting us to a fresh way of seeing things, a new consciousness. He is demanding that we let go of our former defensive dualistic paradigms and make the transition into a new vision of things that is summed up in the metaphor of the 'kingdom of God'.

Jesus through humour exposes and discloses

He uses caricature in order to unmask the true character of the Pharisees:

> Then Jesus said to the crowds and to his disciples, 'The scribes and the Pharisees sit on Moses' seat; therefore, do whatever they teach you and follow it; but do not do as they do, for they do not practise what they teach. They tie up heavy burdens, hard to bear, and lay them on the shoulders of others; but they themselves are unwilling to lift a finger to move them. They do all their deeds to be seen by others; for they make their phylacteries broad and their fringes long. They love to have the place of honour at banquets and the best seats in the synagogues, and to be greeted with respect in the market-places, and to have people call them rabbi.
>
> (Matt. 23.1–7)

Shockingly, he prohibits the use of the word teacher or father: 'But you are not to be called rabbi, for you have one teacher, and you are all students. And call no one your father on earth, for you have one Father – the one in heaven' (Matt. 23.8–10). Charmingly, he calls the Pharisees painted sepulchres:

> Woe to you, scribes and Pharisees, hypocrites! For you are like whitewashed tombs, which on the outside look beautiful, but inside they are full of the bones of the dead and of all kinds of filth. So you also on the outside look righteous to others, but inside you are full of hypocrisy and lawlessness.
>
> (Matt. 23.27–28)

Jesus motivates and energizes new action

Unnerving and disturbing complacency, Jesus uses an image that is ludicrous or even dangerous: 'No one after lighting a lamp hides it under a jar, or puts it under a bed, but puts it on a lampstand, so that those who enter may see the light' (Luke 8.16). In this category we see his saying about hands. Even the most dedicated fundamentalist would not take this literally: 'If your hand causes you to stumble, cut it off; it is better for you to enter life maimed than to have two hands and to go to hell, to the unquenchable fire' (Mark 9.43). It is a joke – with a serious message.

Jesus heartens and cheers his listeners

Jesus uses humour to unsettle us, to enable us to laugh at the absurd and to help us not take ourselves too seriously. His unstuffy teaching concretizes the message of the kingdom: 'why are you bothering with a speck of dust in your brother's eye, when there is a log or a telegraph pole sticking out of your own eye?' (Matt. 7.3; my translation).

A memorable metaphor speaks volumes and there is hope for the follicularly challenged: 'even the hairs of your head are all counted' (Matt. 10.30). And by outrageous exaggeration, Jesus makes a point that will change our lives: '[Forgive your brother] not seven times, but, I tell you, seventy-seven times' (Matt. 18.22).

And then there are the two camel jokes. It seems that Jesus was particularly amused by this awesome animal! 'I tell you, it is easier for a camel to go through the eye of a needle than for someone who is rich to enter the kingdom of God' (Matt. 19.24). Dour scholars want to take the fun out of this hilarious/serious saying by arguing that the 'eye of a needle' refers to a narrow gate in Jerusalem, which camels can't easily pass through. But they miss the point, again. It's a joke – get over it! – you're allowed to laugh!

Jesus also says, 'You blind guides! You strain out a gnat but swallow a camel!' (Matt. 23.24). Jesus is saying that the Pharisees are so preoccupied with the minutiae of the purity laws that they miss the bigger problem, even though it is staring them in the face – like an 'unclean' camel!

71

In our pastoral ministry, permit hilarity, jocularity to break out. A serious message need not be a solemn one!

Crazy actions

As we travel through the Gospels we notice unconventional, pro-vocative and prophetic actions by Jesus, so that his family thought he was insane (Mark 3.21). The Greek means literally 'out of his mind'.

- He comes eating and drinking.
- He picks wheat on the sabbath day.
- He calls a child into the midst of the disciples to teach them about true greatness.
- He celebrates how God reveals the most important things to babies.
- In the midst of the storm on the lake he falls asleep, his head on a cushion.
- He embraces the untouchable leper.
- He allows dubious women to anoint him and to dry him with their flowing hair.
- He positions himself next to the questionable woman at the well.
- He does enigmatic things, such as drawing in the dust.
- He walks on water and invites Peter to join him.
- He makes his solemn entry into Jerusalem seated on an ass!

Our ministry

How does this play out in your ministry? Is there a rightful place for crazy words and crazy actions if they proclaim the kingdom in your context? St Paul gets us started:

> For the message about the cross is foolishness to those who are perishing, but to us who are being saved it is the power of God . . . God's foolishness is wiser than human wisdom, and God's weakness is stronger than human strength.
>
> (1 Cor. 1.18, 25)

St Paul celebrates how God's very strategy, as it were, is based on this clowning and jesting. And if this is God's way, then it also provides the model for our own ministry:

> Consider your own call, brothers and sisters: not many of you were wise by human standards, not many were powerful, not many were of noble birth. But God chose what is foolish in the world to shame the wise; God chose what is weak in the world to shame the strong . . . Do not deceive yourselves. If you think that you are wise in this age, you should become fools so that you may become wise.
>
> (1 Cor. 1.26–27; 3.18)

Henri Nouwen, during a stay in Rome in 1979, noticed that Paul's words ring true today in the practice of Christian ministry:

> Clowns are not in the centre of the events. They appear between the great acts, fumble and fall, and make us smile again after the tensions created by the heroes we came to admire. The clowns don't have it together, they do not succeed in what they try, they are awkward, out of balance, and left-handed, but . . . they are on my side. We respond to them not with admiration but with sympathy, not with amazement but with understanding, not with tension but with a smile. Of the virtuosi we say, 'How can they do it?' Of the clowns we say, 'They are like us.' The clowns remind us with a tear and a smile that we share the same human weakness.[4]

In recent years those responsible for training clergy and lay leaders have rediscovered the image of the clown and jester. In the 1970s Heije Faber noticed how the role of the hospital chaplain resonates with the image of the clown. He pointed out some of the paradoxes in ministry: there is a profound belonging – to the team, to humanity – yet a certain isolation and loneliness in leadership in ministry; being is as important as doing.

In the early 1980s Alastair Campbell took this further. He suggested that the image of minister as clown liberates us from the success ethic that often takes over ministry – the driving conviction that we have to achieve things and get good results. Rather, he suggests, the clown teaches us that presence is as important as activity, and great fruits flow from spontaneity, creativity and playfulness. In 1990 Donald Capps reminded us that the minister, like the clown, helps us see things from a different standpoint. The minister/clown challenges prevailing assumptions and dares to ask questions that slice through complexity and sophistications with a disarming simplicity or naivety. In this way the minister/clown strikes to the heart of the matter. This resonated with the approach of Jesus we noted above. The purpose of humour is not primarily to entertain but to enable transparency and truth-telling.[5]

An example of clowning

The people of my parish of St Peter's East Blatchington were stunned by the response to 'It'. Vanessa Feltz talked about It on her Radio 2 show and the panel discussed It on ITV's *Loose Women*. It was featured on the BBC News website and got on the national news. It got a mention in *The Sunday Times*, in their column Little England, which describes eccentric goings-on in the UK. In fact It was in all the UK daily papers. I was even photographed with It on the front page of the *South Coast Leader*, and interviewed on BBC Radio Five Live. The *Church Times* ran an article with a cartoon, and linked It with something the Archbishop of Canterbury said. It was on Yahoo news. It has even got on to a website called OMG in Ghana and on an Iranian website! I was interviewed live on Israeli radio about It. People were intrigued and baffled by It. My wife fled to her mother's, to escape the paparazzi!

It was the clownish idea of making a CD recording of the silence in our parish church. It sounds like a piece of tomfoolery but was deadly serious, in a quirky way. The CD runs for 30 minutes and begins with a gentle introduction by the rector (myself). The recording of St Peter's atmosphere features the ambient sound of footsteps, voices, background traffic noise – but mostly nothing at all. Robin Yarnton, a church technician at St Peter's, said: 'It does what it says on the tin. Silence is all you get.' Copies have been selling like hot cakes! As the BBC television programme *South East Today* put it: 'Can you believe your ears? The silence CD is a sell-out!'

Like many parish churches across the land, St Peter's has been
a sacred space for more than eight centuries. Of course, it is filled
with sermonic noise, chattering parishioners and good music at
certain times. But we keep the church open from dawn to dusk,
and visitors and locals call in to light a candle and, well, listen.
Listen to the silence.

The CD of recorded silence seems to resonate with what St Paul
said about the foolishness of God confounding the wisdom of this
world. Our society is filled with sound-making gadgetry. We have
tablet PCs, smartphones, MP3 players and so on.

It seems people can't walk along the street without pumping
some noise into their brains. I see folk of all ages walking in the
country lanes or on the South Downs wearing head or earphones
blaring out music (my daughter is an international DJ so I must
be careful what I say here). But I wonder if this continual need to
fill our heads with entertainment is actually a strategy of avoidance,
designed to prevent our being reflective, prevent our confronting
the hard issues of life and death? It has become a way people
protect themselves from facing the deeper issues. They are connected – to noise, music, networks – but weirdly disconnected
from themselves. The stresses and strains mount up – they don't
go away.

That's why buying a CD of silence is a clownish and crazy
idea, it seems. Producing the CD was in a way one of the daftest
things I have done in church. But its countercultural message is
the message of a clown. It subverts and unsettles conventional
attitudes.

There is something paradoxical about silence. It seems an emptiness but reveals a fullness; it seems an absence of something but
affords the chance to sense and experience the palpable presence
of God. Silence feels like something is missing but in fact leads
to finding something precious, making a great discovery. I was
accused by someone of selling blank CDs and I had to correct
them: the CD was full and brimming with the sounds of silence
and with the presence of God.

Other paradoxes surface. Spending half an hour listening
to silence seems like a waste of time but could turn out to be

a big investment, if we get in touch with our deepest selves and in touch with God. It sounds like achieving nothing but through it we could be gaining a fresh perspective on things. Stillness reorientates us and brings space into our chaotic, frenetic lives. The silence of this CD also gives us a chance to catch up with ourselves and get in touch with our truest longings. Like the desert, so important in Christian spirituality, it allows no hiding place. It is a time to be real, real with God and real with ourselves as well. Going into silence might look like escapism from the world but actually turns out to be a needful reality check. There is an immediacy about silence – in it we are plunged into truth, confronted by ourselves and by God. Like the desert, silence can be inviting and threatening, affirming but maybe disturbing. Recently clergy have been speaking to me about this.[6] One said, 'Silence gives oxygen to my soul'; another, 'Silence sorts me out, but I don't understand how that happens.'

Why is it that we do almost anything to avoid silence? Is it its truth-telling quality? Silence can be a scary, intimidating place to be because in it we come, as it were, face to face with God and our own reality. It confronts us with our own aloneness and mortality. But silence – strangely and beautifully – communicates the accepting love of God. It does not judge us or utter pronouncements; it simply holds us in being, just as we are. It enfolds us, embraces us, reassures us that all will be well. And it is also strangely rejuvenating, even healing – perhaps because we are giving God a chance to work on us!

This is a recent example of clowning in my own ministry. My wife even said she would buy a copy of the silence CD because she really needed one. When, I asked, would she listen to it? She said she would get a set of headphones and listen to it when I was talking – again.

Questions for reflection

1 In what ways can you become more playful and spontaneous with words and actions?

2 What would your ministry look like if you modelled yourself on Christ the clown more daringly? What place is there for mirth and merriment in your ministry? In what ways do you permit joviality to break out?
3 How do you utilize humour and jocularity in your ministry now? In what ways does the gospel inspire you to develop this audaciously?
4 Is there an outrageous word or action that you are just longing to share but have kept under wraps? Is God beckoning you to do or say something risqué and risky for the sake of the kingdom?
5 What is stopping you playing the fool, for Christ's sake?

Prayer exercise

Attempt something out of character – something other people wouldn't expect from you. It should preferably have a humorous content, so play the fool, for the sake of the kingdom! Permit yourself to say or do something outrageous, as long as this expresses a theme in the gospel that will cheer or challenge. Release a bit in you that is suppressed, that clamours for expression – unlock it and let it go and create some laughter.

Afterwards, in a time of quiet prayer, reflect on this. How did it make you feel? Did it help you to recognize that humour has a place in sharing the good news?

Further reading

R. Buckner, *The Joy of Jesus: Humour in the Gospels* (Norwich: Canterbury Press, 1993).

H. Cox, *The Feast of Fools* (Cambridge, MA: Harvard University Press, 1969).

M. Frost, *Jesus the Fool: The Mission of the Unconventional Christ* (Peabody, MA: Hendrickson, 2010).

R. W. Funk, *Honest to Jesus* (San Francisco: HarperSanFrancisco, 1996).

J. Maalouf, *Jesus Laughed and Other Reflections on Being Human* (Kansas City, MO: Sheed & Ward, 1996).

B. Manning, *The Importance of Being Foolish: How to Think Like Jesus* (New York: HarperCollins, 2005).

C. Samra, *The Joyful Christ: The Healing Power of Humour* (San Francisco: Harper & Row, 1985).

S. E. Wirt, *Jesus, Man of Joy* (Eugene, OR: Harvest House, 1999).

7

Jesus the iconoclast

Idol-breaking in ministry

———•◦•———

I think it was C. S. Lewis who first called God an iconoclast:

> Images of the Holy easily become holy images – sacrosanct.
> My idea of God is not a divine idea. It has to be shattered time
> after time. He shatters it Himself. He is the great iconoclast.

And he goes on:

> Could we not almost say that this shattering is one of the
> marks of His presence? The Incarnation is the supreme
> example; it leaves all previous ideas of the Messiah in ruins.
> And most are 'offended' by the iconoclasm; and blessed are
> those who are not.[1]

In recent years it has been recognized that Christ was an iconoclast
before he became an icon.[2] Scholars have been noticing how
quickly the earthly and human person of Jesus has been transformed into a remote and sometimes antiseptic dogma. Whatever
might be said about the development of Christian doctrine and
the unfolding of the mystery of Jesus, it has become easy to lose
sight of the dusty first-century teacher who strolled through the
Galilean hills. It is easy to miss the sharp edges in Jesus' teaching
and his radicality. In this chapter we look at how Jesus turned
upside down and inside out many of the religious conventions of
his age. And we will ask: Do we have the courage to name our
idols in our own context? Are we prepared to smash the images
that creep into our lives and ministries today?

What is an idol? It is an idea or custom to which we have come
subservient, to which we bow the knee without thinking. It has

become a false god that we worship or honour – literally, an image that is adored.

The Ten Commandments are emphatic. They begin

> I am the LORD your God, who brought you out of the land of Egypt, out of the house of slavery; you shall have no other gods before me. You shall not make for yourself an idol, whether in the form of anything that is in heaven above, or that is on the earth beneath, or that is in the water under the earth. You shall not bow down to them or worship them; for I the LORD your God am a jealous God.   (Exod. 20.2–5)

Isaiah 44.9–20 scathingly mocks the idol-worshipper, while the psalms express a strong condemnation:

> The idols of the nations are silver and gold,
>   the work of human hands.
> They have mouths, but they do not speak;
>   they have eyes, but they do not see;
> they have ears, but they do not hear,
>   and there is no breath in their mouths.
> Those who make them
>   and all who trust them
>   shall become like them.   (Ps. 135.15–18)

Idols, of course, are not only physical images made of wood or metal. They are any image or idea that has become a false god that has gained respect or honour but is in fact a distortion or perversion of the truth. The most famous iconoclasts, of course, are the Byzantines, who destroyed icons in Constantinople in two waves of attacks in the eighth and ninth centuries – they saw icons as idolatrous graven images. In England iconoclasts in the Reformation destroyed much of the art in churches for the same reason – they saw it as perverting pure religion. Today the word is used of anyone who is prepared to destroy some cherished idea or physical feature they believe is a severe falsification.

Can we see Jesus as an iconoclast? We can recognize at least four major issues where Jesus is concerned to break conventions or destroy cherished ideas.

The destruction of the Temple

First, looking at the mighty walls of the temple sanctuary in Jeru-salem, Jesus foresees their demolition: 'You're impressed by this grandiose architecture? There's not a stone in the whole works that is not going to end up in a heap of rubble!' (Mark 13.2, *The Message*). Jesus the builder and demolition expert, as we noted in Chapter 1, declares: 'Destroy this temple, and in three days I will raise it up' (John 2.19). The greatest icon of God's presence had become the greatest idol and needed to be removed from the very landscape. No greater symbol of Judaism existed than the mighty Temple, recently rebuilt by Herod the Great on the site where Solomon had erected and consecrated the first house of God in about 970 BC.

The Temple is celebrated in the Psalms as the residence of God himself, the locus of his presence: 'How lovely is your dwelling place, O Lord of hosts! . . . For a day in your courts is better than a thousand elsewhere' (Ps. 84.1, 10). But it had become a parody of itself. Instead of being the locus of the Holy of Holies it had become a symbol of exclusion of the unclean, bastion of the self-righteous Pharisee. It seems inviolable, invincible but Jesus sees it as an idol to be knocked over – in the so-called 'cleansing of the Temple' the tables crashing to the ground represented the very walls of God's sanctuary.[3]

The idolatry of the sabbath

Second, the Pharisees were concerned to keep the sabbath day holy, not only because this was prescribed in the Ten Commandments but because it was a 'purity marker' – as the Holy Land was under Roman occupation, such customs helped to preserve and uphold Jewish identity in a contaminated society. But Jesus is not to be bound by custom.

> Again he entered the synagogue, and a man was there who had a withered hand. They watched him to see whether he would cure him on the sabbath, so that they might accuse him. And he said to the man who had the withered hand,

'Come forward.' Then he said to them, 'Is it lawful to do good or to do harm on the sabbath, to save life or to kill?' But they were silent. He looked around at them with anger; he was grieved at their hardness of heart and said to the man, 'Stretch out your hand.' He stretched it out, and his hand was restored. The Pharisees went out and immediately conspired with the Herodians against him, how to destroy him.   (Mark 3.1–6)

Jesus the iconoclast reacts with anger to their hardness of heart – he is furious at the ability of the Pharisees to elevate the sabbath in a way that rules out the healing of the sick. He is unafraid of making provocative actions. His entering the synagogue on the sabbath day and calling forward for healing a man with an injured hand provokes not only criticism but active opposition: 'The Pharisees went out and immediately conspired with the Herodians against him, how to destroy him' (Mark 3.6). Iconoclasm is not for the faint-hearted. In Peter Wallace's view:

Jesus rebels in anger against a power system that holds hurt-ing people hostage. He's not interested in maintaining a set of social or religious norms that thwart the dynamic of God in the world. So he deliberately provokes the religious leaders, intentionally initiating controversy and destabilizing the situation. He rises above anger to offer hope and healing, despite the consequences.[4]

In Matthew 12.9–13 Jesus uses another argument and logic:

Suppose one of you has only one sheep and it falls into a pit on the sabbath; will you not lay hold of it and lift it out? How much more valuable is a human being than a sheep! So it is lawful to do good on the sabbath.

Walking through the fields he plucks and eats grain, as did David, defying the sabbath regulation (Matt. 12.3–4; Mark 2.25–26; Luke 6.3–4; 1 Sam. 21.1–6). He is emphatic: 'The sabbath was made for humankind, and not humankind for the sabbath' (Mark 2.27). Brendan Manning comments: 'He was not only breaking the law, He was destroying the very structure of Jewish society.'[5]

The traditions of the elders

Third, Jesus is prepared to offer a radical critique to the *hallakah*, the interpretations offered by the Pharisees. He observed how they were preoccupied with external cleansings of cup and plate:

> Listen to me, all of you, and understand: there is nothing outside a person that by going in can defile, but the things that come out are what defile ... Do you not see that whatever goes into a person from outside cannot defile, since it enters, not the heart but the stomach, and goes out into the sewer?' (Thus he declared all foods clean.) And he said, 'It is what comes out of a person that defiles. For it is from within, from the human heart, that evil intentions come.
>
> (Mark 7.14–21)

Jesus cuts through punctiliousness and scrupulosity to get to the central issue: where our very heart stands with God.[6]

The lure of wealth

Fourth, 'For where your treasure is, there your heart will be also' (Luke 12.34). This saying about the heart relates to the accumulation of wealth: Matthew reminds us that thieves break in to steal 'treasures on earth' (6.19). Perhaps it was at Sefforis that Jesus first became disgusted by the obscenity of wealth at the cost of the poor. There he saw opulent villas dripping in the trappings of luxury built on land confiscated from poor families, being built by Jewish peasants living at subsistence level. There his anger was kindled, and a protest against wealth – an iconoclastic approach to the gods of mammon – became a recurring theme in his preaching. With the man normally called 'the rich young ruler' Jesus seems to be particularly tough on this issue:

> Jesus, looking at him, loved him and said, 'You lack one thing; go, sell what you own, and give the money to the poor, and you will have treasure in heaven; then come, follow me.' When he heard this, he was shocked and went away grieving, for

he had many possessions. Then Jesus looked around and said
to his disciples, 'How hard it will be for those who have wealth
to enter the kingdom of God!' And the disciples were perplexed
at these words. But Jesus said to them again, 'Children, how
hard it is to enter the kingdom of God!'   (Mark 10.21–24)

Why is Jesus so uncompromising? It is not because the guy has
material acquisitions – it is because these have become an idol,
a focus of devotion and energy. The New Testament seems to have
this message – it is not what you have that matters but what
you do with what you have; how you treat what you have. Jesus
condemns the man who will build great barns to house his
accumulations (Luke 12.18). You cannot serve God and money
(Matt. 6.24). As Jon Sobrino puts it:

Jesus describes idolatry in all clarity . . . For Jesus, the idol is
not a 'religious' idol but an actual reality: *mammon*, wealth.
This is an idol that offers salvation to those who worship
it . . . but a false salvation in Jesus' eyes. And it is an idol that
produces victims through the worship offered to it: the
poor . . . we must hate the idol.[7]

As Sobrino sees it, the wealth Jesus condemns comes at the cost
of the poor. So what *is* an idol? Sobrino affirms: 'idols are not a
thing of the past, nor realities that occur only in the religious
sphere, but currently and really exist: they are actual realities that
shape society and determine the life and death of the masses.'[8]
What is an iconoclast? It is someone who is prepared to smash
the idols; to act radically; to question inherited assumptions and
traditional norms, undeterred by centuries of tradition; to 'think
outside the box' – someone who will not be straitjacketed by
societal bias or prejudice. Jesus does not appear, in this image, as
a gentle reformer or someone who wants to bring a few revisions
to the culture's thinking. Radically, he calls out for 'new wineskins
for new wine'. What does *your* ministry look like in this light?

What do we idealize and idolize? William Cowper's hymn tells
us that 'for a closer walk with God' we must name and shame the
idols in our life:

The dearest idol I have known,
Whate'er that idol be,
Help me to tear it from thy throne
And worship only thee.

The spiritual adventure is a progressive journey into inner freedom, inviting us to a decisive letting go or smashing of the idols. Three vital areas need attention.

False images of God

Even our cherished liturgies can foster a view of God that is akin to an angry, vengeful schoolmaster or a harsh, judging, exacting, punitive bookkeeper who elicits from our hearts a sense of shame and guilt. In the Book of Common Prayer (1662), still widely used, we get prayers like the Confession in Holy Communion: 'Almighty God . . . we acknowledge and bewail our manifold sins and wickedness . . . provoking most justly thy wrath and indignation against us . . . the burden of them is intolerable.'

The Presbyterian Committee on Congregational Song has recently thrown out the popular Evangelical hymn 'In Christ alone' – it was nominated for a new hymnbook but rejected because of its line 'The wrath of God was satisfied.' The Precentor of Salisbury Cathedral had asked: 'Are we really to believe that the angry God, propitiated by a blameless victim, is the God and Father of our Lord Jesus Christ?'[9] And yet the popularity of this hymn in many circles testifies that this distorted image of God is widely respected.

In John's Gospel we get insights into false images of God. John 8 opens with those who would stone a woman for her act of adultery: Jesus will show that he is not able to condemn her. The chapter progresses with a debate between Jesus and the Judeans: Jesus proclaims a God who brings freedom (8.31–36) but the people find themselves in a spiritual bondage. In chapter 9 the disciples reveal that they are trapped in a distorted view of God and sin. They ask Jesus about a man blind from birth: 'Rabbi, who sinned, this man or his parents, that he was born blind?' The disciples imply a belief in God who visits innocent children with the consequences of parents' misdeeds. But Jesus is clear: 'Neither this man nor his parents sinned; he was born blind so that God's works might be revealed in him' (John 9.1–3).

Jesus sees God as accepting Abba, not as an angry, judgemental God. He longs that we enter fully into our baptismal identity and dignity, rejoicing that we are his beloved sons and daughters, with whom he is well pleased. The God of Jesus, revealed for example in the parable of the Prodigal Son, is a God who longs for us, who desires to embrace us, accept us and enfold us in his unconditional love. If we are preaching a different type of deity we may be honouring an idol that deserves to be smashed to pieces. As we noted in Chapter 5, Jesus is one who welcomes at his table of fellowship and friendship the outcast and the impure. So we will decisively reject anything, even in Scripture, that erodes this conviction – especially those Psalms (like 137) that begin with humanity but end with smashing children's heads against the rock!

False views of others

Jesus was prepared to question and overturn the prejudices of his day, such as the conventions that declared women second-class citizens – they were demeaned and marginalized and their testimony was unacceptable in a court of law. Mary Magdalene becomes the first witness of the resurrection. For Jesus, the leper too is to be embraced and accepted, just as the sick – deemed impure and outcast – were welcomed into the Temple (Matt. 21.14). And despised Samaritans are to be welcomed – they it is who teach us the path of courageous compassion (Luke 10.25–37).

In our ministry we may be upholding idols or false ideas that come from the culture of our present-day 'isms' – individualism, consumerism, materialism, sexism, racism, ageism – and the cult of beauty and youth. These can even infect churches and appointments. We must celebrate the awesome dignity and capacity of everyone to bear God in themselves. Indeed, we help people realize that they have the potentiality to be the new temple or residence of God. Richard Rohr puts it: 'The most courageous thing we will ever do is to bear humbly the mystery of our own reality.'[10] Macrina

Wiederkehr prays: 'God, help me to believe the truth about myself, no matter how beautiful it may be.' A false self-image can distort the thinking of clergy and Christian leaders themselves: a sense of self-denigration, putting oneself down and a failure to celebrate one's uniqueness demotivates and sucks the energy out of ministry.

False ideas of ministry

One of the most serious idols I have encountered in Christian leaders is the determination to acquire measurable results that affirm their worth and usefulness. Priests become achievers not receivers. The success mindset, the protestant work ethic, can infect our practice of ministry with guilt.[11] There is even the temptation among some towards ambition, seeing the ministry as a career rather than as an unfolding vocation. Not unrelated to this is a perfectionist view of ministry – an inability to let go and relax, the perceived responsibility of carrying the weight of the world's burdens on our shoulders, a sense of being indispensible to God and his people. Not only can this cause burnout, it can end up maintaining an egocentric view of ministry – a 'What would they do without me?' mentality. There can also be the idol of control freakery, common among the clergy – the desire or need to be in control at all times.[12]

Another false idea that threatens ministry is the obsession that the priest or leader needs to be involved in every activity of the church – and in the process we lose sight of an overarching vision. The episode in the Gadarene country illustrates this powerfully (Mark 5.1–20). Jesus asked the man: 'What is your name?' What is his identity, his character? What makes him tick? The name that comes back is revealing: 'My name is Legion; for we are many.' Jesus meets a man who is fragmented, divided, split up, pulled in so many directions at once. To this divided self Jesus brings a radical reordering – a new centre of gravity, a new centredness and, most of all, a new unity and sense of purpose. At the end of the story Jesus can sum up the new purpose: 'Go home to your friends, and tell them how much the Lord has done for you.' The man receives a unifying sense of mission.

Clergy can identify with the man in the Gospel. What is your name? What is your job? 'Legion!' We are jacks of all trades, jugglers balancing many balls in the air. We are preachers, visitors, carers, organizers, administrators, counsellors, teachers – and so we could go on. Today's word for 'Legion' is 'multitasking'! Our leadership evolves to the extent that we allow Christ to heal our fragmented-ness: as we are pulled this way and that, from one stress to another, we allow Christ to give us, again, a unifying vision. What is the overarching vision and purpose, uniting and integrating your ministry? For Jesus the sole purpose, the unifying vision, the driving force, his only cause is the kingdom of God, the reign of God in people's lives. Matthew puts it: 'Jesus went about ... proclaiming the good news of the kingdom' (9.35). We must pray that the priority of the kingdom will unite our own leadership and displace every idolatry.

A common idol embraced by the clergy concerns, significantly enough, worship – a fixation with certain forms of worship or styles of music that end up becoming straitjackets or security blankets. God calls us to leave our comfort zones sometimes and even risk different expressions of worship and prayer! In my own ministry I encountered a congregation that venerated a certain form of liturgy and displayed an excessive devotion to choir and organ. How was I going to smash this idol? I asked the Churchwarden if she wanted to support the youth. She answered in the affirma-tive. Then I asked her if we could set aside some funds for some percussion instruments – not detailed – for use by young people in church. She said, 'Yes, that sounds like a good idea!' And so the worship band was born – the next day I bought a second-hand drum kit and donated my own guitar so we could get started! An idol, reverenced for many years, had been broken. My father-in-law, an accomplished carpenter, helped to loosen the pews – bolted to the floor – so we could create a space for the new band. No faculty was applied for.

Questions for reflection

1 Are you a conformist or a non-conformist? Why?
2 What is the issue that causes you most pain or discomfort today? What are you prepared to do about it?

3 What is holding you back from smashing icons? Name what is inhibiting you. Fear? Respectability? Are any of these unconquerable?

4 What is your prevailing and usual image of God? How does it look in the light of the themes of this book? Does it need revisiting or revisioning?

5 What is your image of self? In what ways do you celebrate your unique gifting? Are you prepared to smash other people's images of your ministry if they are unrealistic, perfectionist or unduly idealistic?

Prayer exercise

Find a symbolic way of expressing your anger at certain idols: throwing stones into the sea, or more easily at home, write out on a piece of paper your current frustration with God or name the idol that disturbs you. Crush it up into a ball and cast it into a wastepaper bin placed in front of a cross. Let this be a way of throwing at God the frustration you have identified or let this action represent your decisive rejection of the idol you have named. Then spend some moments silently looking at the cross above the bin. See there how Christ enfolds the world's troubles and your own strife. And give thanks.

Further reading

G. Beale, *We Become What We Worship: A Biblical Theology of Idolatry* (Downers Grove, IL: InterVarsity Press, 2008).

T. Keller, *Counterfeit Gods* (London: Hodder & Stoughton, 2010).

D. Linn, S. Fabricant Linn and M. Linn, *Good Goats: Healing our Image of God* (Mahwah, NJ: Paulist Press, 1994).

B. Rosner, *Greed as Idolatry: The Origin and Meaning of a Pauline Metaphor* (Grand Rapids, MI: Eerdmans, 2007).

C. Thomas, *Will the Real God Please Stand up? Healing our Dysfunctional Images of God* (New York: Paulist Press, 1991).

C. J. H. Wright, *The Mission of God* (Downers Grove, IL: InterVarsity Press, 2006).

8

Jesus the revealer and enigma

Epiphany in ministry

————•◆•————

In the next two chapters we explore two Christologies that have particular resonances in the Holy Land today. In Chapter 9 we see how Palestinian Christians have rediscovered Jesus as liberator. Here, our starting point for an exploration of the significance for ministry of Jesus as messiah will be to recall how messianic Jews – Jewish Christians – see Jesus as revealer.

The State of Israel prohibits missionary activity. The Israeli parliament, the Knesset, outlawed any religious proselytization, whether indirect through health care and education or direct by persuasion and witness. However, it is not against the law for an individual to convert. It is estimated that there are about 20,000 messianic Jews in the State of Israel. Several Jewish Christian congregations meet in Jerusalem – some are recognized and gather publicly, others have to meet clandestinely because of local hostility. Some identify themselves as Christians, others as Jews. Appreciating the person of Jesus principally in terms of the revealer/ Messiah, they prompt us to take another look at this Christology. We discover what astonishing and unexpected light this image casts on our practice of priesthood and ministry.

Messianic hope

As we trace the development of messianic hope in the Old Testament and intertestamental period we see how the theme of humanity's longing for a revealer occurs again and again. There is a thirst and desire for someone who will reveal and make plain not only the truth about God but about humanity: 'The people who walked in darkness have seen a great light . . . For a child has been born for us, a son given to us . . . and he is named Wonderful Counsellor' (Isa. 9.2, 6). This great messianic text then goes on to describe the coming deliverer in terms of an idealized successor to King David: 'His authority shall grow continually, and there shall be endless peace for the throne of David and his kingdom' (9.7). The same prophet depicts the coming messiah as one who will reveal new insight into the nature of God: 'The spirit of the LORD shall rest on him, the spirit of wisdom and understanding, the spirit of counsel and might, the spirit of knowledge and the fear of the LORD' (11.2).

The messiah is to be an anointed kinglike figure who will unveil the mystery of God. The hope for a divinely appointed king strengthened during two periods in particular. During the Exile (586–516 BC), when the Israelite population was displaced, the longings for a future deliverer/revealer intensified. Jeremiah looked for a figure who would establish a new covenant (Jer. 31). Ezekiel saw the longed-for saviour in terms of a shepherd-king after the pattern of David (Ezek. 34). Later there was a rekindling of messianic hope when the Jewish people experienced the failure of the Hasmonean kings to uphold peace and justice (152–63 BC). The Essene community at Qumran, on the shore of the Dead Sea, expected two messiahs: a political liberator and a spiritual revealer.

The messianic hope finds its fulfilment in the pages of the New Testament. In the account of the annunciation, Gabriel says to Mary: 'He will be great, and will be called the Son of the Most High, and the Lord God will give to him the throne of his ancestor David' (Luke 1.32). Luke and Matthew locate the birth of Jesus in Bethlehem precisely to affirm that he is the messiah: according to prophecy the messiah has to be born in the City of David. The Pauline writings celebrate the revealing of the mystery: '[God] has made known to us the mystery of his will, according to his good pleasure that he set forth in Christ, as a plan for the fullness of time, to gather up all things in him, things in heaven and things on earth' (Eph. 1.9–10). Paul delights in what has happened: '"What no eye has seen, nor ear heard, nor the human heart conceived, what God has prepared for those who love him" – these things God has revealed to us' (1 Cor. 2.9–10).

Messianic revelation

If we want to know what God is like, we take a long look at Jesus. We see him healing the sick and welcoming the marginalized and we realize that this is our God, a God who excludes no one from his enveloping love. We see Jesus teaching and sharing words of deepest wisdom and we realize afresh how God wants to guide and shape our lives. When we see Jesus stretching out his arms wide on the cross we glimpse the depths of God's love for us. When we discover the risen Christ breaking out of the prison of death we recognize that nothing can defeat or overpower the indestructible grace of God.

This is a great theme running throughout the fourth Gospel: Jesus reveals God in his words of teaching and deeds of power. In his teaching Jesus discloses of the will of God himself:

> Do you not believe that I am in the Father and the Father is in me? The words that I say to you I do not speak on my own; but the Father who dwells in me does his works ... the word that you hear is not mine, but is from the Father who sent me. (John 14.10, 24)

Jesus speaks in symbol and allegory: 'I have said these things to you in figures of speech. The hour is coming when I will no longer speak to you in figures, but will tell you plainly of the Father' (16.25).

Jesus discloses the mystery of God in his miracles, which for John are *signs* manifesting divine glory and *shekinah* presence, pointing to the mystery of eternal life. The greatest place of revelation is, of course, the cross. Here Jesus lays bare the heart of God and cries out at the end, 'It is finished!' (19.30). He affirms: 'I, when I am lifted up from the earth, will draw all people to myself.' John notes: 'He said this to indicate the kind of death he was to die' (12.31–32).

In John's Gospel Jesus not only reveals God, he also reveals the truth about humanity. Jesus unmasks and names the pretence, pride, delusion lurking in the Pharisees (for example in chapter 8). As in Matthew 23, Jesus exposes their hypocrisy. As John notes: 'he knew all people and needed no one to testify about anyone; for he himself knew what was in everyone' (2.24–25).

Unveiling the secrets of the kingdom

When we examine the Synoptic Gospels we detect a similar theme, albeit expressed differently. Jesus says to the disciples: 'To you has been given the secret of the kingdom of God' (Mark 4.11). The Greek word *musterion* denotes something as yet unknown: 'secret, especially of religious matters known only to the initiated'.[1] In Matthew's Gospel the word is the plural *mysteria*: there are many secrets to be discovered (Matt. 13.11). Jesus diverges hidden things and initiates his closest followers into knowledge of the divine – he senses they are ready to receive this revelation. The English word 'reveal' means literally 'to remove the veil'. As the veil separating humanity from the divine – the heavy curtain before the Holy of Holies in the Temple sanctuary – is ripped apart from top to bottom at the time of the crucifixion, so throughout the ministry of Jesus there is an unveiling of the divine. Jesus announces the imminent inbreaking of the reign of God.

In Luke's Gospel we note how Jesus as Messiah reveals God's compassion and acceptance to those who are marginalized. In chapter 15 his parables proclaim the longing of God for people gone astray. Jesus celebrates *apokalupsis* – 'disclosure' or 'revelation' – taking place in the pastoral experience of the Seventy and in his own ministry:

> At that same hour Jesus rejoiced in the Holy Spirit and said, 'I thank you, Father, Lord of heaven and earth, because you have hidden these things from the wise and the intelligent and have revealed them to infants; yes, Father, for such was your gracious will. All things have been handed over to me by my Father; and no one knows who the Son is except the Father, or who the Father is except the Son and anyone to whom the Son chooses to reveal him.' (Luke 10.21–22)

Luke gives us glimpses into the hidden emotional life of Christ. Weeping over Jerusalem, Jesus lays bare the longing of his inmost heart (Luke 19.41–44; 13.34). Luke alone tells us how in Gethsemane Jesus embraces an agony and struggle of mind and spirit (22.44).

When we turn to Mark's Gospel, Jesus is announced as the Messiah in the opening line. This is 'the gospel of Jesus Christ, the Son of God' (1.1, ESV). We encounter a Messiah who makes known God's longing in the calling of the disciples by the water's edge (1.16ff.). He demonstrates the healing love of God as the whole city crowds around the house in Capernaum, seeking cure and relief (1.32ff.). In Mark, Jesus comes to declare the kingdom with urgency:

> 'Let us go on to the neighbouring towns, so that I may pro-
> claim the message there also; for that is what I came out to
> do.' And he went throughout Galilee, proclaiming the message
> in their synagogues and casting out demons.
>
> (Mark 1.38–39)

He instructs the healed demoniac to go home to his friends and tell them what God has done – to open the mystery to others (5.19). This announcing of God's reign leads up to a pivotal moment in the Gospel when Jesus asks: 'who do you say that I am?' (8.29).

This crucial passage introduces us to a second, startling and enigmatic theme in the Gospels. In response to Peter's declaration, 'You are the messiah', Jesus says something stunning and unex-pected: 'And he sternly *ordered* them not to tell anyone about him' (8.29–30). The Greek word has this force and effect: he rebukes Peter, takes him to task, and absolutely forbids him to speak of him. What on earth is going on? The same Jesus who publicly declares and announces the kingdom, the one who proclaims openly and unveils the secrets of God's reign, now strictly insists that the matter is not to be spoken of!

Messianic secret

Jesus in Mark's Gospel appears elusive, intriguing and baffling. There is a sense of obscurity. He is a paradox and an enigma.

He inspires in his followers a sense of wonder and awe: 'They were on the road, going up to Jerusalem, and Jesus was walking ahead of them; they were amazed' (10.32). Repeatedly he tells his hearers *not* to speak of him. He instructs the demons who recognize him to keep silent (1.25, 34; 3.11). He requires that the people he has healed do not publish his name or fame abroad (1.43ff.; 5.43; 7.36; 8.26).[2]

A recurrent theme in Mark is the disciples' confusion and failure (8.17–21; 9.19). They see but do not see (8.18). The mystery of Christ is so wonderful, so potentially overpowering, so astonishing that the disciples can only glimpse the truth little by little – like the blind man at Bethsaida who is healed by Jesus in stages: first he can see only the vague shape of people, looking like walking trees; later he can see everything in clear focus (8.22–26). This becomes a symbol of the disciples' experience – they come to understand the mystery of Jesus gradually. But he has the last word: the Gospel ends on a note of utter bafflement as the women flee from the disturbing empty tomb: 'trembling and astonishment had come upon them' (16.8, RSV). Several times in his Gospel (1.22; 6.2; 7.37; 10.26) Mark tells us that the disciples or hearers were astonished beyond measure. The Greek verb he uses, *ekpleesso*, can convey the sense that one is scared out of one's wits, frightened out of one's senses, utterly astounded or dumbfounded. Using a different, strong word, the disciples are described as 'being beside themselves with astonishment, stupefied'[3] (6.51).

In Mark's Gospel the themes of unveiling and concealing the mystery are interwoven and blended: Jesus is both revealer and enigma. There is so much to be revealed, so many hidden depths, that he will always remain something of a mystery even though he is partially revealed. Does this not say something powerful to us about the nature of priesthood?

Priesthood: revealing – and veiling – the Messiah?

William Countryman expresses the heart of priesthood thus: 'It is the ministry that introduces us to *arcana* – hidden things, secrets . . . The hidden reality of which I speak has many names. It may be

called GOD, the DIVINE, the HOLY, the NUMINOUS.'[4] Paul
expresses his priestly ministry in terms of revealing a long-hidden
mystery:

> I became the servant [of the Church] according to God's
> commission that was given to me for you, to make the word
> of God fully known, the mystery that has been hidden
> throughout the ages and generations but has now been
> revealed to his saints. To them God chose to make known
> how great among the Gentiles are the riches of the glory
> of this mystery, which is Christ in you, the hope of glory. It
> is he whom we proclaim, warning everyone and teaching
> everyone in all wisdom.   (Col. 1.25–28)

Robert Barron brings us to the heart of the matter when he affirms:

> The priest of Jesus Christ is, first and foremost, a mystagogue,
> one who bears the Mystery and initiates others into it. At
> the heart of the Christian faith is a confrontation with the
> all-grounding and all-encompassing mystery of Being itself,
> which is God. The believer is grasped, shaken, overwhelmed
> by that powerful force, which in Jesus Christ is revealed as
> wild, passionate, unconditional love . . . The priest is the one
> who bears that strange power and who leads the people of
> God into an ever more intimate contact with it.[5]

Jesus himself puts it: 'nothing is covered up that will not be uncovered,
and nothing secret that will not become known. What I say to
you in the dark, tell in the light; and what you hear whispered,
proclaim from the housetops' (Matt. 10.26–27). Simeon predicted:
'This child is destined . . . so that the inner thoughts of many will
be revealed' (Luke 2.34, 35). But the fact remains: 'The kingdom
of heaven is like treasure hidden in a field' (Matt. 13.44).

Five vehicles of revelation

First, we recall that in the celebration of the Eucharist the priest
as president draws back the veil between heaven and earth. The
Book of Common Prayer calls the holy communion 'these holy

mysteries' and reminds us that it is with angels, archangels and with the whole company of heaven that we worship the divine: heaven and earth touch, interpenetrate and intersect at the altar. The priest becomes the conduit – the channel through which the risen Christ breaks in once again, appearing in energizing bread and inebriating wine – because it is the priest who says, 'This is my body . . . This is my blood.' One of the challenges for the priest is to celebrate the Eucharist in such a way that the mystery of Christ's radiant presence astounds and astonishes the worshippers, leaving them breathless and wordless:

> Here, O my Lord, I see thee face to face;
> Here would I touch and handle things unseen.[6]

The priest as revealer of the holy is especially clear in the liturgies of the Eastern churches. In the Ethiopian tradition, churches often consist of concentric circles with the holy of holies at the very centre. On the altar are the *tabot* – two consecrated blocks of wood representing the tablets of the Ten Commandments delivered by Moses from Sinai. The Ethiopian priest will position himself on the threshold of the holy of holies and at certain points in the liturgy will push open massive wooden doors, perhaps 6 metres (20 feet) tall, which bear a colourful representation of an angel. Here the priest is literally opening the door to the sacred, and at the end of the liturgy, on certain occasions, he will joyfully bring out the *tabot*, covered in rich cloths and resting on his head – the word of God coming once again, as it were, down the mountain and out into the centre of the community. In the Syriac and Armenian traditions the altar, which stands on a high platform or *bema*, is concealed by a richly decorated heavy curtain. This curtain is withdrawn at certain points of the liturgy so that the worshippers can glimpse heaven as represented in the altar alight with many candles. At these points when the priest pulls back the curtain, the deacons rattle their liturgical fans noisily, representing the presence of the angels. It is a dramatic symbol of the priest as revealer of the holy. In the Byzantine tradition, at the Great Entrance the deacon leads a joyful procession to the altar, bearing the Eucharistic gifts of bread and wine – in a sense already holy as they have been prepared and set aside – as the sixth-century Cherubic hymn is sung:

> We, who mystically represent the Cherubim,
> And chant the thrice-holy hymn to the Life-giving
>   Trinity,
> Let us set aside the cares of life
> That we may receive the King of all,
> Who comes invisibly escorted by the Divine Hosts.[7]

The question remains, however: does the Eucharist conceal or reveal? The hymns are ambiguous, and full of the paradox that surfaces in our ministry:

> O Jesus, by thee bidden,
> We here adore thee, hidden
> In forms of bread and wine.[8]

And yet we may proclaim of the Sweet Sacrament Divine

> in thy far depths doth shine
> thy Godhead's majesty.[9]

With Thomas Aquinas himself we pray:

> O Christ, whom now beneath a veil we see,
> may what we thirst for soon our portion be:
> to gaze on thee unveiled, and see thy face,
> the vision of thy glory and thy grace.[10]

Second, standing at the brink of the baptismal waters, the edge of the liminal space of font or pool, the priest has the awesome privilege of revealing to the candidate his or her own potential in Christ: infant or adult is affirmed as beloved child of God, as *theotokos*, as bearer of God – on them will descend the Spirit of the new creation as they wade through the waters of transformation.

Third, we trust that our teaching ministry will be revelatory. The rediscovery and re-institution of the adult catechumenate in recent years has helped us appreciate again the role of the priest – as catechist – as revealer of the holy. The passage to initiation is expressed as a spiritual journey with four phases: the enquiry stage, looking at the gospel; the catechumenate, examining the creeds; the period of purification and enlightenment or illumination (often coinciding with the season of Lent), introducing the sacraments; the post-baptismal catechesis or mystagogia, emphasizing the task of evangelization.[11] In this journey the candidate is introduced to the 'mystery of faith' by stages. The journey intensifies in the Lenten period when the candidate is taught about the sacraments (viewed as 'the mysteries'), culminating with initiation into the Church at the Easter Vigil through baptism and first Eucharist. The role of priest or catechist is, little by little, to unfold the mysteries, facilitating a deepening experience in the candidates of Christian formation and growth in faith.

Fourth, in preaching, the principal role of the priest or deacon is, indeed, revealer: disclosing to the hearers the secrets of the kingdom. The challenge of the pulpit is that it should become the place of epiphany, the site where revelation happens – in front of which the hearers become dumbfounded with amazement at the love of God – before they go out to proclaim the good news with lips unsealed. In the pulpit we may dare to explore those most mysterious and unfathomable aspects of Christology – the Cosmic Christ, filling all things and sustaining the entire universe (Eph. 1.9–10; Col. 1.17).

Fifth, in the practice of pastoral ministry the priest or deacon discloses the unstoppable and unconditional love of Christ. The pastoral visit becomes the locus of theophany, where God appears through the sacramentality of word or touch. In the situation being faced, the priest longs for the disclosure of the divine; encounter with God amid the pain or confusion. The priest desires to celebrate the sacrament of divine presence in the centre of everyday life so that everything brims with God. The pastoral task becomes the privilege of stimulating and awakening our senses to the presence of mystery; to help people become alert to the divine milieu. Thomas Merton says that the gate of heaven is everywhere – our role is to help open the door. In a sense our task is to roll away the stone and unleash the energy and wonder of the risen Christ. Fr Daniel O'Leary puts it:

Like the poet, the priest sees infinity in an hour, heaven in a pebble, eternity in a smile and divine power in a forgiving word. His vocation is to enable others to see everything that way too . . . the priest is like the spiritual sleuth in search of life-giving clues in a place of confusion; the holy scout with eyes skinned for God's footsteps in a territory of misleading signs and ambiguous symbols . . . a kind of miner who probes the packed soil of our complex existence for the gold that reveals the true source and destiny of our human condition.[12]

John O'Donohue echoes these sentiments:

The intention of priesthood is not to bring people something which they lack and with which you have been exclusively gifted. Rather the priest attempts to kindle in them the recognition of who they are . . . priesthood attempts to awaken the fecundity of being to the possibilities of its own becoming.[13]

In all these ways it is clear that the priest's primary vocation is to be a person of the Holy: 'Think of us in this way, as . . . stewards of God's mysteries' (1 Cor. 4.1). The priest is not social worker, counsellor or sociologist but spiritual leader, revealer of the sacred; opening the door to the holy, unveiling the mystery.

Mystery persists

But while revelation is happening, the priest remains aware that we are standing only on the fringe, the brink of the mystery: it will take a lifetime and an eternity to begin to explore. The priest remains both revealer and enigma, pointing to a world, to a divinity, as yet partially discovered.

Gregory of Nyssa (330–95), one of the Cappadocian Fathers, was the first writer to develop this theme, which was to become an important strand in thinking of spiritual development throughout the history of Christian spirituality.[14] As Jean Daniélou puts it: 'In Gregory of Nyssa . . . the term "darkness" takes on a new meaning and an essentially mystical connotation . . . Gregory's originality

consists in the fact that he was the first to express this characteristic of the highest stages of mystical experience.'[15]

Gregory's ideas are to be found in the context of his account
of the spiritual journey allegorized from the experience of the
people of Israel. In his *Life of Moses* he traces a map of the Christian
pilgrimage as it is suggested to him by the Exodus accounts.[16]
It begins with baptism, prefigured in the crossing of the Red
Sea, liberating a person from the captivity not of Pharaoh but of
sin. The Christian pilgrim's journey, like the trek through the
wilderness, will be marked by God's provision (as in manna,
water from the rock), God's guidance (the pillar of cloud), human
failure and spiritual battles (as represented in the conflict with the
Amalekites). Ultimately all this leads to the ascent of the mountain
of divine knowledge, represented in Sinai: the encounter with
divine darkness. In Moses' first encounter with God, in the Burning
Bush, God appears as light, as illumination. For Gregory, this
represents the beginning of the Christian conversion, a turning
from the darkness of falsehood to the light of Christ. This process
of illumination, for beginners, involves a purification of the soul
from foreign elements. However, as the Christian, like Moses,
progresses along the spiritual journey, he or she is led into
darkness – not a negative darkness but a 'luminous darkness'.
This represents the unknowability of God – this is the apophatic
spiritual path, which falls silent before the unspeakable mystery
of God.

Such writers in the apophatic tradition, walking the *via negativa*,
caution us about being too slick when talking of God. Ultimately
the priest or minister nurtures a sense of wonderment. The priest
cherishes the ineffability of life and is content to rest in the unfathomable love of God, which is beyond comprehension; to taste the
peace of God that 'passeth all understanding'. Perhaps the greatest
task of the priest is to inspire a longing and a thirst in people for
something more – 'Without any doubt, the mystery of our religion
is great' (1 Tim. 3.16).

Recent Church of England research into the thought world of
young people puts it like this: 'At times, the mission of the Church
is to make the truths of God clear, simple and accessible. At other

times the mission of the Church is to spark people's curiosity.'[17] Jesus is both revealer and enigma. The messianic secret persists.

Questions for reflection

1 What does your ministry look like when framed in terms of 'revealing the holy'? What do you make of the affirmation above: 'Perhaps the greatest task of the priest is to inspire a longing and a thirst in people for something more'?
2 How can we celebrate the Eucharist to emphasize the theme of unveiling the sacred, so that the souls of participants might shimmer and quaver in awe?
3 What is your experience of theophany or epiphany in the midst of pastoral visiting?
4 How do you find yourself responding to the affirmation that Jesus is 'paradox and enigma'? How do we show Jesus, messianic revelation and secret, in our own ministry?
5 In what particular ways do you manifest your ministry as a holy man or holy woman?

Prayer exercise

This prayer time is in two phases. First, sit for a while in utter darkness. Let the darkness and silence speak to you of people's longing for God – their deep need for Christ's revelation. Also, as you quieten your heart and silence your lips, pray in the *apophatic* mode – with wordless wonder and no attempt at describing the divine.

Second, when you are ready, light a candle before you. See how the light dispels the darkness. Look at the flame and find yourself praying that you will be a radiant light in the world, revealing the wonder and mystery of Jesus to others. Pray now in the *kataphatic* mode – affirming your love for Christ and attempting to find words to express your wonder. Pray that your light may intensify and burn ever brighter as you yourself discover more of him. Pray that epiphany may take place during your ministry today. End by praying Charles Wesley's great hymn:

O Thou who camest from above,
The pure celestial fire to impart,
Kindle a flame of sacred love
Upon the mean altar of my heart.

There let it for thy glory burn
With inextinguishable blaze,
And trembling to its source return,
In humble prayer and fervent praise.

Jesus, confirm my heart's desire
To work and speak and think for Thee;
Still let me guard the holy fire,
And still stir up thy gift in me.

Ready for all thy perfect will,
My acts of faith and love repeat,
Till death thy endless mercies seal,
And make my sacrifice complete.

Further reading

J. A. Fitzmeyer, *The One Who Is To Come* (Grand Rapids, MI: Eerdmans, 2007).

W. Horbury, *Messianism Among Jews and Christians: Twelve Biblical and Historical Studies* (London: T. & T. Clark, 2003).

P. J. Philibert, *Stewards of God's Mysteries: Priestly Spirituality in a Changing Church* (Collegeville, MN: Liturgical Press, 2004).

D. Power, *A Spiritual Theology of the Priesthood* (Edinburgh: T. & T. Clark, 1998).

9

Jesus the liberator

Setting free in ministry

———••◆••———

Struggles in the Holy Land in the last few years have led Christians to take another look at the image of Jesus the liberator, the one who leads us into freedom. This can be a real stimulus and encouragement for us all in our ministry, whatever context we find ourselves facing. It was in Latin America that this image of Christ was first rediscovered, in the face of oppressions and denial of human rights there. As Jon Sobrino puts it:

> this new image of Christ . . . is what we may call the most important Christological fact in Latin America, a real 'sign of the times' . . . this image better conveys the relevance of Christ for a continent of oppression because it is 'liberating' . . . after five centuries an image of Christ has appeared that is different from and existentially contrary to the traditional one.[1]

As liberation theology developed in the Holy Land, Palestinian Christians began to see Jesus of Nazareth as one who both inspires and empowers the struggle for unfettering those trapped and subjugated by oppressive rule.[2] Broadly, the image of Jesus of Nazareth as liberator invigorates and enables a complementary twofold take on freedom, corresponding to two key Gospel texts.

First, we see how Jesus releases us from inner attitudes – attitudes of heart; from bondages in our thinking – crippling and enslaving mindsets: 'if the Son makes you free, you will be free indeed' (John 8.36).

Second, we see how Jesus empowers us for external action, for engaging with physical oppressions, with good news to the poor as a priority (Luke 4). As we explore this we see how Jesus himself participates in the suffering – he does not assist us as some outside and uninvolved agent but helps us from the inside of our pain and himself walks the way of the cross.

Release from inner captivity

In his dialogue with opponents and seekers in John 8, Jesus identifies and names captivities of mind and heart:

> Then Jesus said to the Jews who had believed in him, 'If you continue in my word, you are truly my disciples; and you will know the truth, and the truth will make you free.' They answered him, 'We are descendants of Abraham and have never been slaves to anyone. What do you mean by saying, "You will be made free"?' Jesus answered them, 'Very truly, I tell you, everyone who commits sin is a slave to sin. The slave does not have a permanent place in the household; the son has a place there for ever. So if the Son makes you free, you will be free indeed.' (John 8.31–36)

The Pharisees represent a defensive and predictable mindset that excludes the possibility that God might be able to act outside of their narrow categories. Jesus says to them: 'You judge by human standards' (John 8.15; RSV gives, in a literal translation, 'according to the flesh'). They cannot conceive of the possibility that the Son of Man will be lifted up (8.28). Their mindset chokes their attitudes and becomes a sinful and negative captivity, tying up their minds.

Jesus the liberator comes to set us free from narrow and negative thinking. He comes to release us from false images of God and from damaging images of humanity and constricted views of human potential. He comes to unbind us from the bondages of guilt and shame and from the distortions wrought in our attitudes by the ego. In the Holy Land this speaks to those who have narrow and exclusivist understandings of the land itself – that it is only for one people and not to be shared in equally. Such attitudes pervert justice and encourage oppression: the inner idea of possessiveness becomes externalized in the physical exclusion of people from the territory. Palestinian Christians find themselves living in oppression under the heavy hand of military rule.

Release from outer captivity

Christians have always suffered the tendency of spiritualizing the earthy message of Jesus. This tendency is present in the Gospels in the key texts of the Beatitudes and Lord's Prayer. Matthew spiritualizes Luke's direct 'Blessed are you who are poor' (6.20) into 'Blessed are the poor in spirit' (5.3); but Matthew, we noted, has 'Forgive us our debts' (6.12) while Luke gives us 'Forgive us our sins' (11.4). Matthew spiritualizes Luke's earthy 'kingdom of God' (6.20) into the 'kingdom of heaven' (5.3). However, there was a physicality to the liberation led by Jesus of Nazareth. The kingdom of God is not an otherworldly spiritual domain but concerns life in this world and faces a conflict with earthly political kingdoms. According to Luke, Jesus begins his ministry with the great announcement of his manifesto drawn from the prophet Isaiah concerning realities in the here and now: 'He has sent me to proclaim release to the captives . . . to let the oppressed go free' (Luke 4.18). Jesus finds great inspiration in this passage. It furnishes him with a set of priorities that will govern his liberating ministry, so that he will be able to commend this report to John the Baptist: 'Go and tell John what you have seen and heard: the blind receive their sight, the lame walk, the lepers are cleansed, the deaf hear, the dead are raised, the poor have good news brought to them' (Luke 7.22). Jesus goes on to teach and practise a gospel that radically embraces all. He has come to break down walls that imprison.

Liberation in the Gospels

As we have seen, for Jesus the open table – where everyone regardless of shame or status has a treasured place – expresses his readiness to smash barriers and social taboos and set people free from constricting and strangling social mores. Jesus overcomes centuries-old social dichotomies between the 'haves' and 'have nots'. His radical acceptance of the other dissolves class distinctions.

Luke introduces the theme of *apsesis* – 'letting go', 'release', 'setting free' – in the song of Zechariah (1.77), and it is a word and theme that occurs throughout the Gospel and Acts. In Luke's Gospel we see how Jesus liberates Levi from his cycle of covetousness and how he releases the Gadarene demoniac from the chains that enslaved him (Luke 8). We witness Jesus calling Zacchaeus to a new life and setting the blind man free from his darkness. The parable of the Prodigal Son sums up vividly Jesus' mission of liberation. One theme recurs: Jesus is not our substitute, doing the things we should be doing, rather he is our exemplar, showing us the way. He is at once liberator and empowerer of liberation.

This theme is echoed in John's Gospel. Jesus refuses to be the stand-in, doing all the work. After his feeding the hungry, the crowd, perhaps led by the Galilean zealots, wanted to crown him as a political messiah, overthrowing the heavy yoke of Roman military oppression (John 6.15). But this was not Jesus' way, to be their saviour in the sense of doing what *they* should be doing and letting them off the hook. Rather he wants to empower the people by means of a non-violent strategy of resistance to the occupying powers.

This strategy is represented most strongly in the Sermon on the Mount. Here the actions proposed by Jesus subvert and turn upside down the Roman protocols. Jesus the liberator releases us from the cycle of violence and retribution. If we follow the way of 'eye for eye and tooth for tooth', we shall not only end up blind but toothless too! Jesus cuts through this cycle of destruction:

> You have heard that it was said, "An eye for an eye and a tooth for a tooth" . . . if anyone strikes you on the right cheek, turn the other also . . . if anyone forces you to go one mile, go also the second mile. (Matt. 5.38–41)

Liberation in the Acts of the Apostles

Scholars agree how Luke–Acts is programmatic: the first Christians are to reproduce in Acts what Jesus does in the Gospel.[3] The Lukan tradition provides clues for a pneumatology of ministry: the Spirit of God animates, energizes and makes possible the liberating ministry of Jesus (Luke 4.18). In Luke the Holy Spirit comes to Jesus when he is at prayer (3.21–22) and Jesus teaches his disciples to pray for the Holy Spirit whom the Father longs to give in response to our searching (Luke 11.13). The risen Christ promises the apostles: 'You shall receive power [*dunamis*] when the Holy Spirit comes, and you shall be my witnesses' (Acts 1.8). Roger Stronstad says:

> In this dominical saying Luke gives his readers the key to interpreting the purpose of the gift of the Spirit, not only to the disciples on the day of Pentecost but also throughout Luke–Acts . . . the gift of the Spirit always results in mission.[4]

When we turn to Acts we notice that miracles of liberation are repeated through the ministry of the apostles. Cripples are set free from their captivity of paralysis (Acts 3; 14.8); people are set free from negative demonic activity (16.16). The narrator is ecstatic:

> Yet more than ever believers were added to the Lord, great numbers of both men and women, so that they even carried out the sick into the streets, and laid them on cots and mats, in order that Peter's shadow might fall on some of them as he came by. A great number of people would also gather from the towns around Jerusalem, bringing the sick and those tormented by unclean spirits, and they were all cured.
>
> (Acts 5.14–16)

The theme of imprisonment and liberation pervades Acts as a thread weaving its way through the whole tapestry. Three times the apostles are set free from physical jails and from actual chains (Acts 5; 12; 16); this is symbolic of their liberating ministry because the incarceration is always followed by a more intense and liberated preaching of the gospel. On each occasion Luke describes the process of gaining liberation very vividly. In Jerusalem, after the apostles were arrested and thrown into prison an angel opens the prison door (5.17–19). They are arrested once again (5.26) and then released (5.40). In Jerusalem too Peter is put in jail and, Luke tells us, his chains fall off and an angel leads him out – past two sets of armed guards! In Philippi the jailer 'put them [Paul and Silas] in the innermost cell and fastened their feet in the stocks' (16.24). Luke gives us a graphic account of the liberating earthquake in which 'all the doors were opened and everyone's chains were unfastened' (16.26). The story concludes with the jailer and his whole household receiving the liberating sacrament of baptism (16.33).

Paul: imprisoned and released

Paul's mission as a Pharisaic persecutor of the Church is summed up repeatedly in Acts in terms of binding the Christians and delivering them to prison (8.3; 9.2, 14, 21; 22.4, 5, 19; 26.10). His goal, by enchaining them, is to prevent the followers of the Way from moving freely to proclaim their message. But Paul finds himself arrested and bound with two chains and brought to the military barracks (21.33–34). He is kept in Herod's prison at Caesarea and, it is noted, 'Felix left Paul in prison' (24.27). Even when Paul is in chains, God is at work:

> I want you to know, beloved, that what has happened to me has actually helped to spread the gospel, so that it has become known throughout the whole imperial guard and to everyone else that my imprisonment is for Christ; and most of the brothers and sisters, having been made confident in the Lord by my imprisonment, dare to speak the word with greater boldness and without fear. (Phil. 1.12–14)

It is under guard that Paul is taken on his eventful voyage to Rome. He is not ultimately free, it seems, until the very last verse of the Acts, which finds Paul 'proclaiming the kingdom of God and teaching about the Lord Jesus Christ with all boldness and without hindrance' (28.31).

Paradoxically, throughout this time Paul finds himself 'bound in the Spirit' (Acts 20.22, RSV), 'a captive to the Spirit' (NRSV). It is from his physical incarceration in Ephesus or Rome that Paul writes to the Philippians a letter that has freedom in Christ as its main theme. Paul is clear that Gentiles do not need to worry about such requirements in the Jewish law as circumcision. Paul's conviction is: 'There is therefore now no condemnation for those who are in Christ Jesus. For the law of the Spirit of life in Christ Jesus has set you free from the law of sin and of death' (Rom. 8.1–2). Indeed, his vision for the freedom God gives is wider still: he expresses the cosmic longing that 'the creation itself will be set free from its bondage to decay and will obtain the freedom of the glory of the children of God' (Rom. 8.21). He celebrates the liberty that the Holy Spirit enables: 'Now the Lord is the Spirit, and where the Spirit of the Lord is, there is freedom' (2 Cor. 3.17).

The liberator becomes the captive

There is a powerful statue of Jesus in Jerusalem at the church of St Peter in Gallicantu, which marks the traditional site of the house of Caiaphas. Jesus is in chains, his hands tightly bound – the liberator becomes the captive, the prisoner. Pilgrims are shown the cell where Jesus was incarcerated. Jesus does not come into the human situation as a miracle worker from outer space, as a drop-in problem solver or as a kind of emergency doctor sorting out a crisis and then nipping off. Rather he comes to share the depths of our pain; he plunges himself into the reality of our suffering and stands in closest solidarity with those who suffer. 'He made captivity itself a captive' (Eph. 4.8). He comes into our very midst and alongside us. In his passion he places himself into the merciless hands of police and soldiers.

In our very midst Jesus suffers today and invites us to discern his features in the faces of those who suffer now. Paul Tillich makes central to his understanding of salvation the idea of God's participation in human pain:

> in the Cross of the Christ the divine participation in existential estrangement becomes manifest ... God participates in the suffering of existential estrangement, but his suffering is not a substitute for the suffering of the creature ... the suffering of God, universally and in the Christ, is the power which overcomes creaturely self-destruction by participation and transformation.[5]

Blaise Pascal wrote: 'Christ is in agony until the end of time.' He falls and rises today among us – finds himself in the dirt and dust, sharing the experience of those whose human rights are trampled on. Today he bleeds as blades of rejection are thrust into human flesh in warfare or violence. Christ walked the way of the cross not solely as 'Jesus of Nazareth', as if he were one solitary, private, individual, rather he walked this way as the new Adam, as everyman/everywoman, representing humanity itself. As 'suffering servant' (Isa. 53.12) he embodied the destiny of a people. As Son of Man he becomes a corporate, inclusive figure, encompassing all, and he calls us to find him in the broken and the downtrodden, to recognize his very presence in those who are hurting (Matt. 25).

This has particular resonance in the Holy Land. As Naim Ateek puts it:

> For Palestinian Christians, the experience of Golgotha is not a distant past or sad memory; it is part of everyday indignity and oppression. Our *via dolorosa* is not a mere ritualistic procession through the narrow streets of the old city of Jerusalem but the fate of being subjugated and humiliated in our own land.[6]

We can also recognize the experience of the Jewish people in the Holocaust as a *via dolorosa*. Christ carries the pains of all humanity in his way of sorrows. A recent conference hosted by the Sabeel Ecumenical Liberation Theology Center in Jerusalem was called Christ at the Checkpoint. This title conveys to us the conviction that today the liberator finds himself in situations of oppression, in the land of his birth and ministry.

Recognizing enslavement today

According to the global slavery index compiled by the charity the Walk Free Foundation, nearly 30 million people are living in slavery across the globe, many of them men, women and children trafficked by gangs for sex work and unskilled labour. In India 14 million are enslaved through bonded labour and debt bondage, while in China 3 million are trapped by forced labour (including domestic servitude), sexual exploitation of women and children and arranged marriage.

What forms of enslavement, public or hidden, exist in our own communities today? How does Christ liberate today through our priesthood and ministry? How can we become liberators? Immediately, of course, we respond to this idea with the reaction that God is the only liberator. But there is a role for priests and ministers to help untie the bonds that constrain; to help unbind people and let them go. We need to be able to recognize what is tightening the spiritual life, what is becoming constrictive. The theme of liberation can bring a fresh focus to all we do, and we realize that we are called to set people free through the worship we lead, the teaching we give, the pastoral care we offer and the outreach we inspire. Four priorities stand out.

Priestly ministries of liberation

We proclaim liberty through healing ministry

Jesus the liberator unshackles us from every negativity. He inspires us to forgive and promote forgiveness. We celebrate the power of Christ's absolution and the healing of memories sets people free from the burden of the years. We teach Christ's emphatic message: 'Forgive us our sins, as we forgive those who sin against us.' The words of the Lord's Prayer become clearer when we read: 'For if you forgive others their trespasses, your heavenly Father will also forgive you; but if you do not forgive others, neither will your Father forgive your trespasses' (Matt. 6.14–15). Jesus is uncompromising: 'Whenever you stand praying, forgive, if you have anything against anyone; so that your Father in heaven may also forgive you your trespasses' (Mark 11.25). Jesus gives us this liberating truth in a vivid image:

> So when you are offering your gift at the altar, if you remember that your brother or sister has something against you, leave your gift there before the altar and go; first be reconciled to your brother or sister, and then come and offer your gift.
>
> (Matt. 5.23–24)

When we choose to forgive others we unlock chains that have bound both us, and them, for years. I have found that more liberating grace flows through the sacrament of forgiveness or confession than in any other place: the creative and courageous decision to forgive someone unilaterally without waiting for their penitence, enabled only by Jesus and encouraged by the priest, dissolves the bitterness of decades and opens a new future.

We need to develop healing ministries that pioneer new routes to reconciliation, releasing the other from captivities. We might reimagine our job and vocation as unbinding, unchaining, unshackling and emancipating people in any kind of captivity or bondage. Our teaching ministry will set people free from negative views about themselves – and negative views of others. Our pastoral ministry will radiate the unstoppable, indefatigable love of Christ: 'Just as I have loved you, you also should love one another' (John 13.34). He has shown us how to love and how to treat our enemies, relentlessly and recklessly:

> 'You have heard that it was said, "You shall love your neighbour and hate your enemy." But I say to you, Love your enemies and pray for those who persecute you, so that you may be children of your Father in heaven.'   (Matt. 5.43–45)

Paul echoes this theme: 'Do not repay anyone evil for evil' (Rom. 12.17). Peter puts it: 'Do not repay evil for evil or abuse for abuse; but, on the contrary, repay with a blessing. It is for this that you were called' (1 Pet. 3.9).

Today, enslaving influences include dehumanizing, judgemental and demeaning attitudes. Many dimensions of oppression persist – intensified by prejudice and fear when people face discrimination because of their gender, sexual orientation, class or the colour of their skin. As the gospel celebrates the worth of every person in the kingdom of God, so healing ministry accepts all, affirms their dignity and worth and liberates from the anxieties and phobias that feed bigotry or exclusive mindsets and prejudices. The task of the priest is to build a community and foster an ecology of welcome and affirmation in and through which churches truly restore dignity to those who have been victimized.

Our hope as priests and pastors is that all can join in Charles Wesley's hymn:

> Long my imprisoned spirit lay,
> Fast bound in sin and nature's night;
> Thine eye diffused a quickening ray –
> I woke, the dungeon flamed with light;
> My chains fell off, my heart was free,
> I rose, went forth, and followed Thee.

We nurture interior freedom through spiritual direction

Not unrelated to the healing ministry is our ministry of spiritual direction or accompanying people on the spiritual journey. One of our key aims here will be to encourage such a freedom in people that they will be totally available to God: freedom is *from* something, to open up new possibilities *for* something. It is a significant theme in the *Spiritual Exercises* of Ignatius of Loyola: Christ's cutting us free from all kinds of attachments that tie us down – false securities, dependencies and addictions. In his 'Fundamental Principle' Ignatius encourages a radical *indifference* – by which he means detachment:

> Man has been created to praise, reverence and serve our Lord God, thereby saving his soul . . . Therefore we need to train ourselves to be impartial in our attitude towards all created reality . . . we do not set our hearts on good health as against bad health, prosperity as against poverty, a good reputation as against a bad one . . . The one thing we desire, the one thing we choose is what is more likely to achieve the purpose of our creating.[7]

In the process of discernment we need to be prepared to go either way with a particular choice or decision – achieving a sense of inner freedom marked by a state of equilibrium where we can face both alternatives: 'the one thing I must look at is what I was created for, which is the praising of our Lord God and the saving of my soul'.[8] In giving spiritual direction the priest or pastor encourages people to identify and name their fears or inordinate attachments and begin the process of letting go. We encourage honest self-knowledge. We help people spot their defences and support them as they start to take apart – or create chinks in – self-protective walls fencing them off from others and from God. We encourage people to release their grip on the unnecessary baggage they are carrying. We assist people in recognizing their need to be in control or always right – daring to ask: What does this mean? How does this impact our relationship with God? Through our counsel, Jesus is truly liberator. We might also begin this process of letting go with our own souls.

We celebrate a meal of liberation

This is the key theme of the Last Supper but is often missed altogether in Eucharistic celebrations that derive from it. The Exodus is, of course, the primordial act of liberation in the Bible, and the Passover celebrates the moment of release from Pharaoh's tyranny. The instructions are precise. The celebration is to include the traditional *haggadah*, the words of interpretation:

> 'And when your children ask you, "What do you mean by this observance?" you shall say, "It is the passover sacrifice to the LORD, for he passed over the houses of the Israelites in Egypt, when he struck down the Egyptians but spared our houses."' And the people bowed down and worshipped.
>
> (Exod. 12.26–27)

Jesus gives a stunningly alternative *haggadah* at the Last Supper's Passover meal and thereby reveals what he thinks about his impending death. Taking the paschal elements of bread and wine into his hands, he gives them a meaning we might render as:

> This cup, with which you are expecting to recall the Exodus, is my blood to be shed for you. This unleavened bread, which you are expecting to use to recall the eve of liberation, the night before the great escape to freedom, is my body to be broken for you.

Jesus affirms that the cross will make possible a new exodus into freedom – not from the tyranny of a pharaoh but from humanity's greatest enemies: death and sin. A new deliverance is at hand. In Luke's account Jesus, in the transfiguration event, had spoken with Moses himself about the exodus he would accomplish in Jerusalem (Luke 9.31). The Christian Passover meal, the Eucharist, should clearly proclaim these great themes of liberation, exodus, the new journey into freedom.

We empower others for courageous struggle

The Eucharist we celebrate together should resource, inspire and hearten those who go out into the world to fight against ignorance and prejudice that breed injustice or partiality. We proclaim and live the upside-down kingdom, the kingdom where things seem back to front. Our teaching reflects our lifestyle. We proclaim by word and deed the kingdom values of radical, mutual acceptance in Christ. A main focus of priestly ministry will be to support and cheer those who are in the front line of the struggle upholding human dignity and protesting against unjust social structures. Our teaching and encouraging of spirituality should empower men and women to go out and break down barriers between people – yes, share the liberating love of Jesus of Nazareth.

Jesus the liberator leads us from fatalism to hope. In the Holy Land deterministic attitudes create pessimism among Arab Christians as well as Muslims: they repeat the mantra '*Insha'Allah*' – 'If God wills it'. This can engender a spirit of resignation in the face of oppressions. But Christ leads us through such negative thinking and destroys a spiral of gloom. Paul cheers us:

> If God is for us, who is against us? . . . Who will separate us from the love of Christ? Will hardship, or distress, or persecution, or famine, or nakedness, or peril, or sword? . . . I am convinced that [nothing] in all creation, will be able to separate us from the love of God.   (Rom. 8.31, 35, 38–39)

In 2009 Jerusalem church leaders identified five signs of hope bubbling up in Palestine–Israel. The Kairos document tells us that people of good will are:

1 creating vibrant parish communities where young people are active apostles for justice and peace;
2 strengthening ecumenism and working together across historic divides;
3 advancing interreligious Christian–Muslim–Jewish dialogue, breaking down walls that separate people;
4 maintaining a steadfastness (*samud*) and faithfulness;
5 nurturing a determination to overcome the resentments of the past and strive for reconciliation.[9]

Jesus of Nazareth, Jesus the liberator, conquering the ultimate captivity of death, opens up new pathways to the future. The body of a dead Jesus is transformed into a dynamic rising unfettered Jesus, bursting from the tomb, going ahead to Galilee (Mark 16.7). Jesus is on the loose! He cannot be held down! He opens new futures for us. He empowers and energizes daring ministries of liberation. As Leonardo Boff puts it:

> The resurrection is a process that began with Jesus and will go on until it embraces all creation. Wherever an authentically human life is growing in the world, wherever justice is triumphing over the instincts of domination, wherever grace is winning out over the power of sin . . . wherever hope is resisting the lure of cynicism or despair, there the process of resurrection is being turned into a reality.[10]

Questions for reflection

1 How does the theme of liberation play out in your ministry? Are there any inner attitudes in yourself that have become crippling or captivating?
2 Who in your community are trapped or find themselves in some kind of captivity? Name the unfreedoms they face, outer and inner; addictions or cycles of behaviour that enslave them.
3 How can modelling your ministry on Jesus the liberator redefine your priorities?
4 How can the Eucharist be celebrated more clearly as a meal of liberation?

5 What are the next practical steps you can take to resource and empower people in the front line of struggling for justice?

Prayer exercise

As you reflect on people or situations facing a loss of freedom, compose a litany of intercession along these lines:

> Jesus, liberator, *through me* set free the lonely and isolated. Jesus, compassion, *through me* draw close to those shackled by illness and to the imprisoned housebound.

And so on.

Further reading

P. Casaldáliga and J. M. Vigil, *The Spirituality of Liberation* (Tunbridge Wells: Burns & Oates, 1994).

M. H. Ellis, *Revolutionary Forgiveness* (Waco, TX: Baylor University Press, 2000).

M. Linn, S. Fabricant and D. Linn, *Healing the Eight Stages of Life* (Mahwah, NJ: Paulist Press, 1988).

G. Muller-Fahrenholz, *The Art of Forgiveness: Theological Reflections on Healing and Reconciliation* (Geneva: World Council of Churches, 1997).

A. Nolan, *Jesus Today: A Spirituality of Radical Freedom* (Maryknoll, NY: Orbis Books, 2006).

J. Philippe, tr. H. Scott, *Interior Freedom* (New York: Scepter Publishing, 2007).

A. Wingate, *Free to Be: Discovering the God of Freedom* (London: Darton, Longman & Todd, 2000).

10

Jesus the traveller

Risk and pilgrimage in ministry

———◆•◆•◆———

Soon after the resurrection, according to Acts, Peter describes and sums up his experience with Jesus in a vivid, startling phrase. He refers to 'the time that the Lord Jesus went in and out among us' (Acts 1.21). This phrase captures the dynamic of Jesus' journeys. He was always crossing boundaries, in and out of one place or another.[1]

Notice how often in the Gospels Jesus is in movement, in motion. Jesus in the Gospels is radically itinerant – he doesn't settle down in his three-year ministry but is always on the move. Indeed, 'the Son of Man has nowhere to lay his head' (Luke 9.58). Jesus is a pilgrim and wayfarer. In a sense, perhaps, he was a vagabond – which is defined by the online *Oxford English Dictionary* as a nomadic person who wanders from place to place, without a settled home. According to Matthew, Jesus became a traveller and an exile at just a few days old, a refugee crossing the border into Egypt.

Mark emphasizes Jesus' travels: seven times he uses the phrase 'on the way' or 'on the road' – a symbol of the journey of discipleship.[2] We picture Jesus as a thirsty and dusty (Luke 10.11) explorer, exhausted at times by his trek in the heat, and as a dedicated pilgrim, prepared to walk hundreds of miles to complete his journeys. Luke tells us about Jesus' pilgrimage to Jerusalem at age 12, while John gives us accounts of his pilgrim visits to the Temple for Tabernacles (Succoth) and Dedication (Hanukkah), as well as the Passover celebrations in the holy city.

The Jewish scholar Geza Vermes characterizes Jesus as an itinerant Jewish charismatic,[3] while Martin Hengel explores the extent to which Jesus was a wandering rabbi.[4] Scholars have seen significance in the fact that Jesus is often on the road.[5] If Jesus had remained in Capernaum and set up a base there for his healing ministry, establishing a centre of ministry in Peter's house (Mark 1.38), this would have limited the scope of his ministry and encouraged the growth of a hierarchy requiring a reciprocal relationship between patrons (suppliers) and clients (those seeking healing) – a normal feature of first-century life in Galilee. It is possible that other healers at this time set up healing sanctuaries that developed into a local personality cult. Jesus refuses this option: by staying on the road he opens the kingdom to a diversity of people throughout the region and does not localize the range of lives he will touch and transform.

In his ministry he is peripatetic, always roving. He says: 'today, tomorrow, and the next day I must be on my way' (Luke 13.33). And he is ever leading his disciples into liminal space – across borders, through boundaries, into a risky place where they will be radically changed.

In the Gospels we see Jesus leading the disciples across the mountains of the north, to Tyre and Sidon, to the Mediterranean Sea, exposing them not only to the sea breezes but to new horizons in every sense (Mark 7). Leaving behind the comfort zone of 'home', inherited prejudices, stereotypes and complacencies, the disciples discover new, unsettling and disturbing ways of seeing things; new ways of doing things; an alternative world view, represented in the Gentile Syrophoenician woman.

Later, the disciples quit Capernaum's shoreline of safety, crossing the demon-filled sea to the other side, place of the Gadarene demoniacs. Jesus leads his disciples into enemy territory – into the pagan, heathen, Gentile and foreign cities of the Decapolis (Matt. 4.25).

We notice how Jesus takes his disciples across the desert in his final journey to Jerusalem (there is no other way between Jericho and the holy city). Here in these marginal lands of the Judean desert the disciples discover it to be a place of raw beauty, a wild place where the wind blasts unmercifully at times and a place where they must be real with God.

Jesus takes his disciples across the numinous threshold of the Mount of Olives, climbing up this eschatological/end-time mount (Zech. 14), the very brink of the holy city. In Jerusalem Jesus will lead his disciples on journeys that culminate in the way of the cross, the *via dolorosa* and the pathways of resurrection. Three transitions seem especially relevant to the practice of ministry.

Journey across the Jordan

As Jesus leaves the family home of Nazareth at the start of his adventure and finds himself standing in the waters of the swirling Jordan river, we recall that he not only enters the water but crosses it, from east to west.[6] He is experiencing the bereavement and exhilaration of leaving familiar things behind, moving out to a place where he is not known. What does that mean for us who would follow him?

We experience the pain of bereavement, coupled with a sense of dislocation, when a move is required away from familiar ways and cherished communities of support. We may need to let go of ties to a former community in which we had a deep sense of belonging. On ordination, the loss of privacy as one moves from being a private citizen to public property and into a representative role can be experienced as a painful bereavement of former freedoms. There can be a loss of self-determination: one is no longer one's own but a servant of the Church. There may be the experience of stress as a diversity of new demands can often be felt as perplexing or even overwhelming.

Jesus' passage through the waters of the Jordan speaks power-fully to the transitions that clergy and Christian leaders must make when they take steps forward into new ministries. God's promise echoes across the centuries: 'Do not fear, for I have redeemed you; I have called you by name, you are mine. When you pass through the waters, I will be with you' (Isa. 43.1–2).

Jesus' passage also recalls Joshua's crossing of the Jordan (Josh. 3) at precisely the same place – indeed, Jesus positions himself here to enact a new exodus and a new journey into freedom. At the first entry of the people into the land in these waters we see the priests standing in the place of risk and danger, stepping out into the swirling currents of the Jordan in front of God's people. They bear the Ark of the Covenant; carry the sacred symbol of God's will; are bearers of the sacred, the Holy – the Scripture, the divine Commandment. They carry with them the very power of God. And they are asked to tread first into the racing waters. They are required to be people of faith – big faith – for they believe the waters will cease when they place their feet in the torrent.[7]

We need priests and Christian leaders today who will take God's people across thresholds, beyond boundaries, into uncharted waters, into unexplored lands. In that first crossing of the Jordan it is the priests who play such a crucial role, prepared to pave the way – trailblazers who dare to go first. Such priests are prepared for risk-taking, ready to lead their people from the front – and yet they also bring up the rear, for they will not leave the waters until the last person has crossed. This gives us a vivid image and symbol of those called to be pastors and leaders, who need to walk not only beside God's people but courageously before them, and lead the way across the choppy waters.

Journey into Samaria

A second journey of Jesus inspires the practice of ministry today. We see Jesus entering with the disciples the no-go area, the place of heretics called Samaria. Jesus is presented as a thirsty pilgrim, a needy fellow traveller. The whole story of John 4 reads like a case study in the practice of priesthood and ministry.

Notice how Jesus situates himself *beside* the woman. He does not stand over against her but rather the account is vivid and emphatic: 'Jesus, tired out by his journey, was *sitting* by the well' (John 4.6). He is on the same level as her and is looking yearningly into the ancient well, symbol of humanity's spiritual longing. Jesus is present to the woman as a pilgrim who is himself thirsting. He speaks with directness – there is no beating about the bush, rather clarity and precision: 'Give me a drink'; 'If you knew the gift of God' (4.7, 10). He goes on to affirm the woman as someone worthy of bearing the living water of the Spirit. However much traditional village values might ostracize her or the disciples reject her (4.27), Jesus emphatically declares that she has the capacity to discover an inner spring of the Spirit. He honours her potentiality.

Jesus allows her to ask questions. He does not quench her curiosity or questioning spirit. Three immediately bubble up from her: 'How is it . . . ?' (4.9); 'Where do you get . . . ?' (4.11); 'Are you greater . . . ?' (4.12). Jesus has created a climate of trust in which she is comfortable in sharing her questions, which come straight from her soul. But he is prepared to question her. He challenges her over the issue of relationships (4.16–18). He challenges her view about where one should worship (4.21). 'You worship what you do not know' (4.22). Jesus speaks the truth: 'you have had five husbands, and the one you have now is not your husband' (4.18). There is no avoidance of sensitive issues, no no-go areas. Jesus cuts to the quick. He is aware that the conversation is leading the woman to a place of vulnerability, but it is also a place of honesty and reality.

He teaches her. He gives theological input over the issue of true worship (4.23–24). Finally he empowers her. While the conversation reveals the woman's weakness and need, it also equips her and gives her confidence to proclaim the saviour of the world. She is able to become a powerful witness to her community. As Kathleen Fischer puts it: 'Jesus calls her from the margin to the centre of life, from someone judged unworthy by the tradition, to a role as bearer of revelation to her community.'[8]

Journeys into the unknown

Jesus the traveller and pilgrim inspires priests and leaders to keep moving in their spiritual journey. A dynamic view of the Christian vocation emerges in the writings of Gregory of Nyssa, one of the outstanding theologians of the Eastern Church, who lived in Cappadocia in the fourth century. He communicated an exciting vision of the Christian life as continually evolving and progressing, energized by the Holy Spirit. His key text was the resolve of Paul: 'forgetting what lies behind and straining forward to what lies ahead, I press on towards the goal for the prize of the heavenly call of God in Christ Jesus' (Phil. 3.13–14). Here Paul implies that there is no room for self-satisfaction in ministry. We should never stand still but continually stretch ourselves towards the 'upward call'.

In Gregory's thought, God invites us to make Christian ministry an adventure, in which we are beckoned to keep on growing. Gregory urges us to break free from any way of life that seems deterministic and predictable; to jump off the treadmill of dull routine that traps us into going round in circles. He encourages us to discover our full potential in Christ:

> the finest aspect of our mutability is the possibility of growth in good ... let us change in such a way that we may constantly evolve towards what is better, being transformed from glory into glory, and thus always improving and ever becoming more perfect by daily growth.[9]

For Gregory, each stage we reach in the spiritual journey is but a beginning, not an end – we can never say we have arrived. Every mountaintop we reach, Gregory teaches, is not an opportunity to rest on our laurels but gives us a vantage point from which to see other peaks that summon us.

In the Song of Solomon, Gregory sees a powerful allegory of the relationship between God (the bridegroom) and the Christian (the bride). The bridegroom is a dynamic figure, ever in movement: 'Look, he comes, leaping upon the mountains, bounding over the hills. My beloved is like a gazelle' (Song of Sol. 2.8–9). What is his message to his bride as she relaxes and rests on her couch? 'My beloved speaks and says to me, "Arise, my love, my fair one, and come away"' (2.10). He repeats this call again (2.13). Gregory comments:

> For this reason the Word says once again to his awakened Bride: *Arise*; and when she has come, *Come*. For he who is rising can always rise further, and for him who runs to the Lord the open field of the divine course is never exhausted. We must therefore constantly arouse ourselves ... for as often as He says *Arise* and *Come*, He gives us the power to rise and make progress.[10]

In this image Gregory sees a powerful metaphor for the Christian vocation. We are not to allow ourselves to become too content with where we are spiritually. We are not to rest in our achievements in a spirit of self-congratulation. God ever calls us to the next stage of our development in ministry. Every point of arrival is to be a springboard that catapults us into another adventure! We must keep moving. For this, Gregory teaches, we need more and more of the divine Spirit in our lives. He pictures the Holy Spirit as a Dove who not only broods over our life but actually gives us wings to fly, never staying put for long on the mountain but ever ascending: 'the soul keeps rising higher and higher, stretching with its desire for heavenly things "to those that are before" as the Apostle tells us, and thus it will always continue to soar ever higher.'[11]

The journeys of Jesus invite us and summon us to explore unfamiliar terrain in the practice of ministry; step out of our comfort zones; enter risky spaces – spaces that might turn out to be transformative!

Questions for reflection

1 After reading this book, to what new challenge do you sense God calling you?
2 What is holding you back from stepping out into a risky space with God?
3 A question from the Jordan: how have you experienced the blend of bereavement and exhilaration in a move in ministry?
4 A question from Samaria: have there been no-go areas in your ministry? Why? Who is the Samaritan woman in your context now? How will you get to meet her?
5 What does your ministry look like when you view it through the lens of a pilgrimage or adventure?

Prayer exercise

Review the journey or pilgrimage of your life. On a piece of paper draw a personal timeline (draw a horizontal line and mark it into the decades of your life). Above the line note major events and transitions, including new jobs, housemoves, births and deaths, new ministries. Below the line try to note how you felt at these moments of change. How did you experience God at these moments? Bring this to a close by giving thanks for God's providence in your life, and entrust your future odyssey to him.

Further reading

U. T. Holmes III, *Spirituality for Ministry* (Harrisburg, PA: Morehouse, 2002).

D. J. O'Leary, *New Hearts New Models: A Spirituality for Priests Today* (Blackrock, Co. Dublin: Columba Press, 1997).

P. J. Philibert, *Stewards of God's Mysteries: Priestly Spirituality in a Changing Church* (Collegeville, MN: Liturgical Press, 2004).

M. Riddell, *Godzone: A Guide to the Travels of the Soul* (Oxford: Lion, 1992).

11

Jesus the mentor, brother, trailblazer

Solidarity in ministry

There is one image of Jesus emerging in Gospel research that is very relevant to this study: Jesus as mentor. Scholars have noticed that Jesus is training and preparing his followers for mission so that disciples can become apostles – literally those 'sent out'. The research has observed how Jesus acts as a coach in encouraging his disciples and passing on vital skills, and that there is a place in the Gospels for *imitatio Christi*: Jesus is a model to his disciples. What is the relevance of such an image to this study? It means that we are to allow Jesus to train us today. We are to let these images we have identified – builder, hermit, rebel, mystic, reveller, dancer, jester, iconoclast, traveller – shape our own ministry today.

Jesus – a mentor?

In his monumental study *A Marginal Jew: Rethinking the Historical Jesus*, John Meier indeed characterizes Jesus as a mentor to the disciples.[1] Marcus Borg has spoken of Jesus as a spiritual mentor and teacher of wisdom.[2] Bruce Chilton names his book *Rabbi Jesus*.[3] William Lunny analyses Jesus' ministry of educating the disciples in terms 'training sessions'.[4] Martin Hengel considers this issue when he asks if Jesus the teacher can be viewed as a rabbi: is this the way we should view Jesus' instruction of his disciples?[5]

Jesus is often greeted as a teacher – *didaskolos* – in the narrative but there are certainly a number of instances where he is called a rabbi. At the beginning of the story, John gives us: 'When Jesus turned and saw them following, he said to them, "What are you looking for?" They said to him, "Rabbi" (which translated means Teacher), "where are you staying?"' (John 1.38). At the transfiguration Peter cries out: 'Rabbi, it is good for us to be here' (Mark 9.5).

Hengel notes significant differences between the practice of Jesus and the behaviour of rabbis in first-century Judaism. The usual pattern was for a potential disciple to seek out a rabbi and ask permission to join his teaching group. Jesus breaks this convention and himself calls and summons diverse individuals, often with the invitation 'Follow me'. Hengel does not want Jesus to be forced into the technical mould of a rabbi instructing students within his school, in which the aim of the pupil is ultimately to become a famous teacher himself. It was the aim of rabbinical students, the followers of first-century rabbis, to assimilate to their teachers – by spending long hours in their company to learn their ways, their words and deeds, hoping to become like them. A popular blessing expressing this was: 'May you be covered in the dust of your rabbi.' It seems that this was also the goal of Jesus' disciples.

But while there are differences between Jesus and the image of a traditional rabbi, one thing is clear: Jesus as a teacher is committed to train his disciples – they might even be viewed as apprentices, learning on the job, not unlike Elisha learning from Elijah.[6] In his study *The Teaching of Jesus: Studies of its Form and Content*, Thomas Manson put it thus:

> Jesus was their Master not so much as a teacher of right doctrine, but rather as a master-craftsman whom they were to follow and imitate. Discipleship was not matriculation in a Rabbinical College but apprenticeship to the work of the Kingdom.[7]

In the Gospels the word used for disciples is *mathetes*. Gerhard Kittel points out that '*mathetes* always implies the existence of a personal attachment which shapes the whole life of the one described as *mathetes*, and which in its particularity leaves no doubt as to who is deploying the formative power.'[8] Jesus empowers and equips his disciples as they observe and participate in his very lifestyle and approach to ministry, and expects a kinship and copying to go on in the process: 'A disciple is not above the teacher, nor a slave above the master; it is enough for the disciple to be like the teacher, and the slave like the master' (Matt. 10.24–25). Michael Wilkins, after his study of patterns of learning in the ancient near east, concludes:

> The commitment assumed the development of a sustained relationship between the follower and the master, and the relationship extended to imitation of the conduct of the master. This is the notion of the word [*mathetes*] understood by a Greek audience at the time of the writing of the New Testament.[9]

In Mark's Gospel the Twelve are chosen 'to be with him, and to be sent out' (3.14), for a learning process and an apostolate. Early on Jesus chooses a small team – Peter, James and John – who are given privileged access to his way of working and healing behind closed doors (Mark 1.29; cf. 5.37; 9.2). In the first part of Mark the Twelve learn by observation of Christ's healing and teaching techniques, and at an early stage are sent out in pairs (6.7). In Mark 8, in the journey together towards Jerusalem, Jesus invites his disciples to copy him; to take up their cross and follow him (8.34). Ernest Best notes: 'There is thus here the beginnings of an *imitatio Christi* theology.'[10]

This perspective is echoed in Luke's account, and the missions of the Twelve and the Seventy reveal key aspects of the mentoring process. First there is a period of intense training, which includes listening to Jesus, studiously watching his pastoral approach in the marketplace (Luke 7.32) and in the home and sharing meals with outcasts. Then the Twelve are sent out (9.2) and report back to Jesus (9.10). Next Jesus withdraws with them to a place apart – a 'lonely place' (9.12, RSV) – for a time of shared reflection about their experience, as we noted in Chapter 2.

This pattern is repeated in the experience of the Seventy, sent out in pairs (Luke 10.1) for a ministry of preaching the kingdom and healing, modelled on Christ's. On their return there is reflection, debriefing and feedback on the exercise (10.17–20). Robert Banks identifies four elements in this process:

1 induction: the disciples hear the basic message;
2 observation and participation: they are drawn into helping with Christ's hands-on ministry;
3 modelling: Jesus exemplifies patterns of ministry;
4 fellowship: the experience of being together in a learning community, including debriefing and reflection.[11]

Clearly Jesus emerges as a mentor and coach. The features of his ministry are to be reproduced and developed in that of his followers, through all time.

More than a rabbi – a brother

Jesus is not a mentor in any sense in which he stands above us in instructional mode or on a pedestal. He is a brother to us. It is no accident that the Gospels begin the account of Christ's ministry with his baptism in the River Jordan. Baptism declares a washing away of sin and a readiness to repent. So why does Jesus need baptism? A dumbfounded John protests and tries to prevent him, saying, 'I need to be baptized by you, and do you come to me?' (Matt. 3.14). Jesus embraced baptism to declare his radical solidarity with ordinary men and women. In submitting to baptism he declares himself to stand *among* and not *over against* humanity in its search for God. His baptism proclaims that he is indeed Emmanuel, 'God is with us' (Matt. 1.23), coming to lead us into his kingdom from the inside of our condition, not from the outside. His baptism declares that God really has become one of us.

In Matthew's Gospel Jesus calls his disciples his own brothers: 'pointing to his disciples, he said, "Here are my mother and my brothers! For whoever does the will of my Father in heaven is my brother and sister and mother"' (Matt. 12.49–50; see also Mark 3.33). We discover Jesus as our brother when we do God's will. Paul and other writers suggest that Jesus is the eldest brother: 'the firstborn within a large family' (Rom. 8.29). The Letter to the Colossians puts it: 'He is the image of the invisible God, the firstborn of all creation' (Col. 1.15), while Hebrews assures us that Jesus is our brother:

For the one who sanctifies and those who are sanctified all have one Father. For this reason Jesus is not ashamed to call them brothers and sisters, saying, 'I will proclaim your name to my brothers and sisters, in the midst of the congregation I will praise you.' . . . Since, therefore, the children share flesh and blood, he himself likewise shared the same things . . . he had to become like his brothers and sisters in every respect, so that he might be a merciful and faithful high priest in the service of God . . . brothers and sisters, holy partners in a heavenly calling, consider that Jesus, the apostle and high priest of our confession, was faithful to the one who appointed him.   (Heb. 2.11–12, 14, 17; 3.1–2)

Trailblazer

The author of Hebrews sees a radical affinity and solidarity between Jesus and God's people. This is emphasized by the depiction of Jesus as *archegos*: 'pioneer' (Heb. 2.10; 12.2), trailblazer, groundbreaker – someone who cuts a way forward to enable others to follow. The *archegos* is the leader, the one who shows the way. As William Barclay put it:

the really peculiar meaning of *archegos* is that it regularly describes someone who originates and initiates something into which others can follow. The *archegos* is the first to do something or to discover something, but the characteristic of his action and his discovery is that it opens a way for others to enter into the same benefits and the same greatness . . . The pioneer goes first that others may walk in his steps.[12]

This is underlined by the naming of Jesus as *prodromos* – 'forerunner' (Heb. 6.20). In what context is Jesus the one who goes ahead of us? It is in the context of ministry and priesthood: 'Jesus, a forerunner on our behalf, has entered [heaven], having become a high priest for ever according to the order of Melchizedek' (6.20).

This resonates with the service of ordination where, as we noted in the Introduction, Jesus is set forth as the model of ministry: 'They are to set the example of the Good Shepherd always before them as the pattern of their calling.'[13] We have seen in this book that Jesus is indeed a model, an exemplar, someone to copy in the practice of ministry, but in rather different senses. We have discovered him as builder, teaching us about creativity and courage in leadership. We found Jesus to be both hermit and mystic, perhaps stumbling upon the very secret of his ministry, in energizing silence and solitude in leadership. We explored how Jesus in the practice of his ministry can be understood as both reveller and dancer, telling us something about the place of festivity in leadership. And Jesus the jester allowed us to laugh again as we teach. Jesus revealed himself to us as something of a rebel and iconoclast, unafraid to act and speak in a prophetic and subversive way when needed. And we recognized Jesus as traveller, leading us on risky pathways in our ministry.

The author of the Letter to the Hebrews makes an astonishing and stunning affirmation in his conclusion. In the midst of the vicissitudes and dangers of the present world, he says, 'Jesus Christ is the same yesterday and today and for ever' (13.8). In these words that same author is telling us Jesus dances, revels and laughs today; in these words asking us in the twenty-first century: Do you want to find an exemplar and model for ministry today? Jesus Christ will always stand before you as your brother, trailblazer and pilgrim. In our ministry, then, we have before us an archetype, a pattern, a paradigm, precedent and ideal. He is not a substitute or stand-in for us; rather he empowers us to minister to others as he did. Therefore 'let us run with perseverance the race that is set before us, looking to Jesus, the pioneer and perfecter of our faith' (12.1–2). Paul invites us to 'have the same mindset as Christ Jesus' (Phil. 2.5, NIV).[14] For our own age, and to respond to the needs of today, let us dare to be 'another Christ'.

Questions for reflection

1 Which of the images of Jesus in this book most resonates with your present experience?
2 Are there other images of Jesus that you find relevant to the practice of Christian ministry?

3 After completing this book, how do you summarize the personality and character of Jesus?

4 If Jesus is your mentor, your rabbi, desiring that you become like him, which of the pictures of Jesus most challenges you? Why?

5 How do you feel when you call Jesus not only your model and exemplar but also your brother?

Prayer exercise

What do you want to say to God about the state of your ministry – about your leadership style, the character or theme of your ministry? Are you happy with things as they are or do you sense that God is nudging you towards different expressions of ministry? Tell God what image of Jesus in the present study attracts you most. Visualize yourself acting in this mode or style. Finally, ask for the grace riskily to incorporate this into your present ministry. Give thanks that ministry is not static or determined but something evolving and unfolding.

Further reading

W. J. Harrington, *Jesus Our Brother: The Humanity of the Lord* (Mahwah, NJ: Paulist Press, 2010).

M. Hengel, *The Charismatic Leader and his Followers* (Eugene, OR: Wipf & Stock, 2004).

W. L. Lane, *Hebrews: A Call to Commitment* (Peabody, MA: Hendrickson, 1985).

Notes

Introduction

1 C. Marmion, tr. Dom Matthew Dillion, *Christ: The Ideal of the Priest* (San Francisco: Ignatius Press, 2005). It emphasized the sacrificial aspects of Christ and the priesthood.

2 J. Ziesler, *Paul's Letter to the Romans* (London: SCM Press, 1989), p. 227.

3 A recent restatement of this is in Congregation for the Clergy, *Directory on the Ministry and Life of Priests* (London: CTS, 1994).

4 Eucharistic Prayer F, in Archbishops' Council, *Common Worship* (London: Church House Publishing, 2000).

5 Archbishops' Council, *Common Worship: Ordination Services* (London: Church House Publishing, 2006).

6 For example, J. Adair, *The Leadership of Jesus* (Norwich: Canterbury Press, 2001); R. M. Schwartz, *Servant Leaders of the People of God: An Ecclesial Spirituality for American Priests* (New York: Paulist Press, 1989); J. Adair and J. Nelson (eds), *Creative Church Leadership* (Norwich: Canterbury Press, 2004); J. Finney, *Understanding Leadership* (London: Darton, Longman & Todd, 1989).

7 W. H. Willimon, *Calling and Character: Virtues of the Ordained Life* (Nashville, TN: Abingdon Press, 2000), p. 99. Though writing from a US context, his words seem apposite for English clergy.

8 A. D. Mayes, *Holy Land? Challenging Questions from the Biblical Landscape* (London: SPCK, 2011) and *Beyond the Edge: Spiritual Transitions for Adventurous Souls* (London: SPCK, 2013).

9 H. Anderson, 'Christology: Unfinished Business', in J. H. Charlesworth and W. P. Weaver (eds), *Earthing Christologies: From Jesus' Parables to Jesus the Parable* (Valley Forge, PA: Trinity Press International, 1995), pp. 82–3).

10 C. S. Lewis, *The Lion, The Witch and The Wardrobe* (London: Harper-Collins, 2009).

11 For example, J. Nelson (ed.), *Leading, Managing, Ministering: The Task of Leadership in the Church* (Norwich: Canterbury Press, 1999); R. J. Banks and B. M. Ledbetter, *Reviewing Leadership: A Christian*

Evaluation of Current Approaches (Grand Rapids, MI: Baker Academic, 2004); B. Hughes, *Leadership Toolkit* (Crowborough: Monarch Books, 1998); W. C. Wright, *Relational Leadership: A Biblical Model for Leadership Service* (Carlisle: Paternoster, 2000).

12 Justin Welby in his first presidential address to the General Synod, 5 July 2013: 'Quinquennial Goals for the General Synod 2012–15'.

1 Jesus the builder

1 Later the villas were decorated with stunning frescos and mosaics.

2 The site of Sefforis was for centuries a Palestinian Arab village, until their homes were destroyed and they were expelled by Israeli forces in 1948–9. Patterns of conquest, destruction and rebuilding continue.

3 Indeed, little wood construction went on as it was a scarce resource, unlike the plentiful rock of the land.

4 Jesus quotes Jeremiah 7.11 at the 'cleansing of the temple' in Mark 11.17.

5 See, for example, N. T. Wright, *Jesus and the Victory of God* (London: SPCK, 1996).

6 M. Biddle, G. Avni et al., *The Church of the Holy Sepulchre* (New York: Rizzoli, 2000).

7 The Gospel accounts of the first Easter specifically mention rock. There is the tomb itself that Joseph of Arimathea had had cut into the rock cliff (*petra*). There is the mighty rock or *lithos* that attempted to seal the tomb of Christ and was blasted away in the resurrection events (according to Matthew – parts are preserved in the antechamber of the tomb today in the Altar of the Angels).

2 Jesus the hermit

1 Benedict acknowledges his debt to Basil in his own Rule, which became the basis of western monasticism.

2 All the quotations from Basil are from 'Letter 2' in G. Barrois (tr.), *The Fathers Speak* (New York: St Vladimir's Seminary Press, 1986).

3 The extracts are drawn from A. D. Mayes, *Spirituality in Ministerial Formation: The Dynamic of Prayer in Learning* (Cardiff: University of Wales Press, 2012) and used with permission.

4 The letter following each extract identifies the category of speaker used for the purposes of the study. Newly ordained clergy (ordained 2002–5): (*a*) female, single, twenties, catholic, catholic college, stipendiary; (*b*) male, married, fifties, central, course, NSM; (*c*) female,

single, forties, catholic, course, stipendiary permanent deacon; (*d*) female, married, forties, central, NSM; (*e*) male, married, twenties, evangelical, evangelical college, stipendiary; (*g*) female, married, forties, evangelical, evangelical college, stipendiary. Staff member/tutor: (*m*) male, forties, course.

5 W. L. Lane, *The Gospel According to Mark* (Grand Rapids, MI: Eerdmans, 1974), p. 81.

6 J. D. G. Dunn, *Jesus Remembered* (Grand Rapids, MI/Cambridge: Eerdmans, 2003), p. 561.

7 G. Claxton, *Hare Brain, Tortoise Mind: Why Intelligence Increases When You Think Less* (London: Fourth Estate, 1997), p. 12.

8 For a useful introduction to this pattern of praying, see T. M. Gallagher, *An Ignatian Introduction to Prayer: Scriptural Reflections According to the Spiritual Exercises* (New York: Crossroad, 2008).

3 Jesus the rebel

1 S. H. Lee, *From a Liminal Place: An Asian American Theology* (Minneapolis, MN: Fortress Press, 2010), p. 47.

2 See E. Bammel and C. F. D. Moule (eds), *Jesus and the Politics of his Day* (Cambridge: Cambridge University Press, 1984).

3 P. Walker, *Jesus and his World* (Oxford: Lion, 2003), p. 30.

4 See, for example, J. D. Crossan, *Jesus: A Revolutionary Biography* (San Francisco: HarperCollins, 1995); A. Richardson, *The Political Christ* (London: SCM Press, 1973); O. Cullmann, tr. G. Putnam, *Jesus and the Revolutionaries* (New York: Harper & Row, 1970). Cullmann holds that Jesus was an 'eschatological radical'. See also M. Hengel, tr. W. Klassen, *Was Jesus a Revolutionist?* (Philadelphia, PA: Fortress Press, 1971) and M. J. Borg, *Jesus, a New Vision: Spirit, Culture, and the Life of Discipleship* (London: SPCK, 1993).

5 R. Horsley, *Jesus and Empire: The Kingdom of God and the New World Disorder* (Minneapolis, MN: Fortress Press, 2002); *The Prophet Jesus and the Renewal of Israel: Moving Beyond a Diversionary Debate* (Grand Rapids, MI: Eerdmans, 2012).

6 S. Freyne, *Jesus, a Jewish Galilean: A New Reading of the Jesus Story* (London: T. & T. Clark, 2004).

7 This phrase derives from Crossan, *Jesus: A Revolutionary Biography*.

8 There is a scholarly debate about the nature of Jesus as prophet. Wright sees Jesus as an apocalyptic prophet who embodies the very presence of Israel's God; Sanders as one of a series of Jewish

eschatological prophets. See N. T. Wright, *Jesus and the Victory of God* (London: SPCK, 1996) and E. P. Sanders, *The Historical Figure of Jesus* (London: Penguin, 1993).

9 Liddell and Scott, *Greek–English Lexicon* (Oxford: Clarendon Press, 1974).

10 For this insight I am indebted to M. J. Borg and J. D. Crossan, *The Last Week: A Day-by-Day Account of Jesus's Final Week in Jerusalem* (San Francisco: HarperCollins, 2006), pp. 1–30.

11 R. J. Sider, *Rich Christians in an Age of Hunger: Moving from Affluence to Generosity* (London: Hodder & Stoughton, 1990).

12 See S. Hauerwas and W. H. Willimon, *Resident Aliens* (Nashville, TN: Abingdon Press, 1989); M. L. Buddle and R. W. Brimlow (eds), *The Church as Counterculture* (Albany, NY: State University of New York Press, 2000); B. A. Harvey, *Another City: An Ecclesiological Primer for a Post-Christian World* (Harrisburg, PA: Trinity Press International, 1999).

13 J. Dear, *Jesus the Rebel: Bearer of God's Peace and Justice* (Lanham, MD: Sheed & Ward, 2000), p. 29.

14 P. Casaldáliga and J. M. Vigil, *The Spirituality of Liberation* (Tunbridge Wells: Burns & Oates, 1994), p. 103.

15 Justin Welby, Presidential Address to General Synod, 5 July 2013, <www.archbishopofcanterbury.org/articles.php/5098/there-is-a-revolution-archbishop-justins-address-to-synod>.

16 R. Williams, *Faith in the Public Square* (London: Bloomsbury, 2012).

17 The Archbishops' Council, *Common Worship: Ordination Services* (London: Church House Publishing, 2006).

18 J. Wallis, *The Soul of Politics: A Practical and Prophetic Vision for Change* (London: Fount, 1994), pp. 38, 47.

4 Jesus the mystic

1 J. G. S. S. Thomson, *The Praying Christ: A Study of Jesus' Doctrine and Practice of Prayer* (London: Tyndale Press, 1959).

2 B. Chilton, *Rabbi Jesus* (London: Image/Doubleday, 2002), p. 175. For a more cautious approach to the prayer of Jesus, see O. Cullmann, tr. John Bowden, *Prayer in the New Testament: With Answers from the New Testament to Today's Questions* (London: SCM Press, 1995).

3 M. J. Borg, *Jesus, a New Vision: Spirit, Culture, and the Life of Discipleship* (San Francisco: Harper & Row, 1987), as discussed in M. A. Powell, *The Jesus Debate: Modern Historians Investigate the Life of Christ* (Oxford: Lion, 1998).

4 T. Wright, *Luke for Everyone* (London: SPCK, 2004), p. 125.
5 J.-C. Barreau, 'Preface' in O. Clement, *The Roots of Christian Mysticism* (London: New City, 1993), p. 8.
6 C. P. M. Jones, 'Mysticism, human and Divine', in C. Jones, G. Wainwright and E. Yarnold (eds), *The Study of Spirituality* (London: SPCK, 1986), p. 19.
7 K. Rahner, *Concern for the Church – Theological Investigations, Vol. 20* (New York: Crossroad, 1981), p. 149.
8 E. Underhill, *Mystics of the Church* (Cambridge: James Clarke, 1925), p. 9.
9 Quoted in W. P. Alston, *Perceiving God: The Epistemology of Religious Experience* (Ithaca, NY: Cornell University Press, 1991), p. 25.
10 B. Witherington, *Jesus the Seer: The Progress of Prophecy* (Peabody, MA: Hendrickson, 1999).
11 B. J. Malina, *The New Testament World: Insights from Cultural Anthropology* (Louisville, KY: John Knox Press, 1981); J. P. Meier, *A Marginal Jew: Rethinking the Historical Jesus* (New York: Doubleday, 1991).
12 R. Rohr, *Naked Now: Learning to See as the Mystics See* (New York: Crossroad, 2009), p. 77.
13 R. McAfee Brown, *Spirituality and Liberation: Overcoming the Great Fallacy* (London: Hodder & Stoughton, 1988).
14 J. Macquarrie, *Two Worlds are Ours: An Introduction to Christian Mysticism* (Minneapolis, MN: Fortress Press, 2005).
15 Centring prayer is a recent example of a way of praying in the West, welcoming a renewed sense of the indwelling God and opening oneself up to the divine action within, healing all dichotomy. It was popularized by Basil Pennington and Thomas Keating and promoted by Contemplative Outreach. See M. B. Pennington, *Centering Prayer: Renewing an Ancient Christian Prayer Form* (Garden City, NY: Doubleday, 1980); T. Keating, *Intimacy with God: An Introduction to Centering Prayer* (New York: Crossroad, 2009).
16 Justin Welby, Presidential Address to General Synod, 5 July 2013, <www.archbishopofcanterbury.org/articles.php/5098/there-is-a-revolution-archbishop-justins-address-to-synod>.
17 R. E. Barron, 'Priest as Bearer of the Mystery', in K. S. Smith (ed.), *Priesthood in the Modern World: A Reader* (Franklin, WI: Sheed & Ward, 1999), p. 96.
18 R. Frost, 'Evangelism Beyond the Fringes', in S. Croft, R. Frost et al., *Evangelism in a Spiritual Age: Communicating Faith in a Changing Culture* (London: Church House Publishing, 2005).

5 Jesus the reveller

1 J. D. Crossan, *Jesus: A Revolutionary Biography* (San Francisco: Harper-Collins, 1995).

2 M. J. Borg, *Jesus, a New Vision: Spirit, Culture, and the Life of Discipleship* (London: SPCK, 1993), p. 101.

3 Borg, *Jesus, a New Vision*, p. 133.

4 Brother Roger, *Struggle and Contemplation* (London: SPCK, 1973), p. 31.

5 P. Casaldáliga and J. M. Vigil, *The Spirituality of Liberation* (Tunbridge Wells: Burns & Oates, 1994), p. 29.

6 This section is indebted to Andrew D. Mayes, 'Priestly Formation', in T. Ling and L. Bentley (eds), *Developing Faithful Ministers: A Practical and Theological Handbook* (London: SCM Press, 2012).

7 C. Irvine, *The Art of God: The Making of Christians and the Meaning of Worship* (London: SPCK, 2005), p. 85.

8 Brother Roger, *Festival* (London: SPCK, 1974), pp. 15, 16, 131; adapted to inclusive language.

6 Jesus the jester

1 Harvey Cox's study inspired John-Michael Tebelak, the author of the musical *Godspell*, to celebrate the ministry of Jesus in Matthew's Gospel, in terms of the clown.

2 R. W. Funk, 'Jesus: A Voice Print', in R. W. Hoover (ed.), *Profiles of Jesus* (Santa Rosa, CA: Polebridge Press, 2002), p. 12.

3 See R. Rohr, *The Naked Now: Learning to See as the Mystics See* (New York: Crossroad, 2009) and C. Bourgeault, *The Wisdom Jesus: Transforming Heart and Mind – A New Perspective on Christ and His Message* (Boston, MA: Shambhala, 2008).

4 H. J. M. Nouwen, *Clowning in Rome* (New York: Image Books, 1979), p. 2.

5 H. Faber, 'The Circus Clown', A. V. Campbell, 'The Wise Fool' and D. Capps, 'The Wise Fool Reframed' are reprinted in R. C. Dykstra (ed.), *Images of Pastoral Care: Classic Readings* (St Louis, MO: Chalice Press, 2005). See also H. Faber, 'Second Thoughts on the Minister as a Clown', in *Journal of Pastoral Psychology*, vol. 28 no. 2 (1979), pp. 132–7.

6 Wearing my 'spirituality adviser' hat I have been asking clergy, in their chapters, what is helping their prayer.

7 Jesus the iconoclast

1 C. S. Lewis, *A Grief Observed* (London: Faber & Faber, 1961), p. 55.
2 See, for example, R. W. Funk, *Honest to Jesus* (San Francisco: Harper-SanFrancisco, 1996).
3 N. T. Wright, *Jesus and the Victory of God* (London: SPCK, 1996).
4 P. Wallace, *The Passionate Jesus* (Woodstock, VT: SkyLight Paths, 2013), p. 80.
5 B. Manning, *The Ragamuffin Gospel* (Sisters, OR: Multnomah, 2005), p. 57.
6 We must be careful to note that Jesus' approach was nuanced and sometimes paradoxical: there are sayings in Matthew's Gospel that no doubt reflect the concerns of Matthew's community; some speak of the deepest respect for Judaism and the desire for it to be fulfilled not abolished (Matt. 5.17–18).
7 J. Sobrino, *Jesus the Liberator: A Historical-Theological Reading of Jesus of Nazareth* (Tunbridge Wells: Burns & Oates, 1994).
8 Sobrino, *Jesus the Liberator*, p. 185.
9 *Church Times*, 9 August 2013.
10 R. Rohr, *Everything Belongs* (New York: Crossroad, 2003), p. 97.
11 This is uncovered in the research reported in Society of Mary and Martha, *Affirmation and Accountability* (Dunsford: Society of Mary and Martha, 2002).
12 See J. A. Sanford, *Ministry Burnout* (London: Arthur James, 1982).

8 Jesus the revealer and enigma

1 M. Zerwick and M. Grosvenor, *A Grammatical Analysis of the Greek New Testament, Vol. 1* (Rome: Biblical Institute Press, 1974), p. 111.
2 It was Wrede, of course, who first observed this. W. Wrede, *The Messianic Secret in the Gospels* (London and Cambridge: James Clarke, 1971).
3 Zerwick and Grosvenor, *Grammatical Analysis of the Greek New Testament, Vol. 1*, p. 126.
4 L. W. Countryman, *Living on the Border of the Holy: Renewing the Priesthood of All* (Harrisburg, PA: Morehouse, 1999), pp. 3, 6.
5 R. E. Barron, 'Priest as Bearer of the Mystery', in K. S. Smith (ed.), *Priesthood in the Modern World: A Reader* (Franklin, WI: Sheed & Ward, 1999), p. 94.
6 Hymn by Horatius Bonar, 1808–89.
7 The Cherubic Hymn has been in the public domain since the sixth century. This translation comes from <http://orthodoxwiki.org/

Cherubic_Hymn>. See also J. Raya, *Byzantine Liturgy* (Tournai: Société Saint Jean l'Evangelist, 1958). A composition from the Liturgy of St James appears in our hymn books as 'Let all Mortal Flesh Keep Silence'.

8 Latin, seventeenth century, tr. A. Riley. Copyright owner untraced.

9 F. Stanfield, 1835–1914.

10 T. Aquinas, 1227–74, trans. J. R. Woodford (1820–85).

11 The titles of the different periods of catechesis are taken from the International Commission on English in the Liturgy, *Rite of Christian Initiation of Adults* (London: CTS, 1974). For an Anglican adaptation see P. Ball and M. Grundy, *Faith on the Way: A Practical Parish Guide to the Adult Catechumenate* (London: Mowbray, 2000).

12 D. J. O'Leary, *New Hearts, New Models: A Spirituality for Priests* (Dublin: Columba Press, 1997), pp. 57–8.

13 J. O'Donohue, 'The Priestliness of the Human Heart', in *Way Supplement*, 83 (1995), p. 46.

14 Werner Jaeger has traced Gregory's influence in the life of the Eastern Church:

> It was Gregory of Nyssa who transferred the ideas of Greek *paideia* in their Platonic form into the life of the ascetic movement that originated during his time in Asia Minor and the Near East and that soon was to display an undreamed-of power of attraction.

W. Jaeger, *Early Christianity and Greek Paideia* (Cambridge, MA: Belknap, 1961), p. 100.

15 Jean Daniélou, 'Introduction', in H. Musurillo (tr.), *From Glory to Glory: Texts from Gregory of Nyssa's Mystical Writings* (London: John Murray, 1962), p. 27.

16 See A. J. Malherbe and E. Ferguson (trs), *Gregory of Nyssa: The Life of Moses* (New York: Paulist Press, 1978), II:226.227.

17 S. B. Savage, S. Collins-Mayo et al., *Making Sense of Generation Y: The World View of 15–25-Year-Olds* (London: Church House Publishing, 2006), p. 117.

9 Jesus the liberator

1 J. Sobrino, *Jesus the Liberator: A Historical-Theological Reading of Jesus of Nazareth* (Tunbridge Wells: Burns & Oates, 1994), pp. 12–13.

2 Sabeel Ecumenical Liberation Theology Center, Jerusalem led the way. See N. Ateek, *Justice and Only Justice: A Palestinian Theology of Liberation* (Maryknoll, NY: Orbis, 1989).

3 See, for example, M. Prior, *Jesus the Liberator: Nazareth Liberation Theology (Luke 4.16–30)* (Sheffield: Sheffield Academic Press, 1995); D. M. Sweetland, *Our Journey with Jesus: Discipleship According to Luke–Acts* (Collegeville, MN: Liturgical Press, 1990).

4 R. Stronstad, *The Charismatic Theology of St Luke* (Peabody, MA: Hendrickson, 1984), p. 80.

5 P. Tillich, *Systematic Theology: Part III* (London: SCM Press, 1978), pp. 175–6.

6 Sabeel, *Contemporary Way of the Cross: A Liturgical Journey along the Palestinian Via Dolorosa* (Jerusalem: Sabeel Ecumenical Liberation Theology Center, 2005).

7 *The Spiritual Exercises of St Ignatius Loyola*, tr. T. Corbishley, (Wheathampstead: Anthony Clarke, 1973), paragraph 23.

8 *Spiritual Exercises*, paragraph 169.

9 *A Moment of Truth: A Word of Faith, Hope, and Love from the Heart of Palestinian Suffering* was agreed by the leaders of the historic churches in Jerusalem in 2009; see <www.kairospalestine.ps>.

10 L. Boff, *Way of the Cross – Way of Justice* (Maryknoll, NY: Orbis, 1980).

10 Jesus the traveller

1 This chapter contains extracts from A. D. Mayes, *Beyond the Edge: Spiritual Transitions for Adventurous Souls* (London: SPCK, 2013), where I explore this theme in greater detail.

2 See Mark 8.27; 9.33–34; 10.17, 32, 52.

3 G. Vermes, *Jesus the Jew* (London: SCM Press, 2001).

4 M. Hengel, *The Charismatic Leader and His Followers* (Eugene, OR: Wipf & Stock, 2004).

5 See J. D. Crossan, *Jesus: A Revolutionary Biography* (San Francisco: HarperCollins, 1995), pp. 99–101.

6 He starts on the east bank at Bethany-beyond-Jordan (John 1.28) and crosses to the west bank to enter the Judean desert.

7 See L. W. Countryman, *Living on the Border of the Holy: Renewing the Priesthood of All* (Harrisburg, PA: Morehouse, 1999).

8 K. Fischer, *Women at the Well: Feminist Perspectives on Spiritual Direction* (London: SPCK, 1989), p. 47.

9 H. Musurillo (tr.), *From Glory to Glory: Texts from Gregory of Nyssa's Mystical Writings* (London: John Murray, 1962), pp. 51–2.

10 Musurillo, *From Glory to Glory*, p. 191.

11 Musurillo, *From Glory to Glory*, p. 57.

11 Jesus the mentor, brother, trailblazer

1 J. Meier, *A Marginal Jew: Rethinking the Historical Jesus. Vol. 1: The Roots of the Problem and the Person; Vol. 2: Mentor, Message, and Miracles* (New York: Doubleday, 1991).

2 Referred to in M. J. Borg, *Meeting Jesus Again for the First Time: The Historical Jesus and the Heart of Contemporary Faith* (San Francisco: HarperCollins, 1994), p. viii.

3 B. Chilton, *Rabbi Jesus* (Image/Doubleday, London, 2002).

4 W. J. Lunny, *The Sociology of the Resurrection* (London: SCM Press, 1989).

5 M. Hengel, *The Charismatic Leader and His Followers* (Eugene, OR: Wipf & Stock, 2004).

6 The role of the rabbis really developed after the fall of the Temple in AD 70: this marks the beginning of rabbinical Judaism. Hence it can be anachronistic to compare later descriptions with the ministry of Jesus.

7 Quoted in M. J. Wilkins, *Following the Master: A Biblical Theology of Discipleship* (Grand Rapids, MI: Zondervan, 1992), p. 93.

8 G. Kittel (ed.), *Theological Dictionary of the New Testament* (Grand Rapids, MI: Eerdmans, 1977), p. 441.

9 Wilkins, *Following the Master*, p. 78.

10 E. Best, *Following Jesus: Discipleship in the Gospel of Mark* (Sheffield: JSOT, 1981), p. 39. Cf. processes of interaction between Jesus and the disciples, allowing for reflection, identified in V. K. Robbins, *Jesus the Teacher: A Socio-Rhetorical Interpretation of Mark* (Philadelphia, PA: Fortress Press, 1984).

11 R. J. Banks, *Reenvisioning Theological Education* (Grand Rapids, MI: Eerdmans, 1999), p. 104.

12 W. Barclay, *Jesus as They Saw Him* (London: SCM Press, 1962), p. 344.

13 Archbishops' Council, *Common Worship: Ordination Services* (London: Church House Publishing, 2006).

14 Paul develops such an idea in terms of the 'mind of Christ': 'for "Who has known the mind of the Lord so as to instruct him?" But we have the mind of Christ' (1 Cor. 2.16, NIV).

Did you know that SPCK is a registered charity?

As well as publishing great books by leading Christian authors, we also . . .

. . . **make assemblies meaningful and fun for over a million children** by running www.assemblies.org.uk, a popular website that provides free assembly scripts for teachers. For many children, school assembly is the only contact they have with Christian faith and culture, and the only time in their week for spiritual reflection.

. . . **help prisoners become confident readers** with our easy-to-read stories. Poor literacy is a huge barrier to rehabilitation. Prisoners identify with the believable heroes of our gritty fiction, but questions at the end of each chapter help them to examine their choices from a moral perspective and to build their reading confidence.

. . . **support student ministers overseas in their training**. We give them free, specially written theology books, the International Study Guides. These books really do make a difference, not just to students but to ministers and, through them, to a whole community.

Please support these great schemes: visit www.spck.org.uk/support-us to find out more.